TWENTIETH CENTURY
INTERPRETATIONS

MAYNARD MACK, *Series Editor*
Yale University

NOW AVAILABLE
Collections of Critical Essays
ON

THE ADVENTURES OF HUCKLEBERRY FINN

ALL FOR LOVE

THE FROGS

THE GREAT GATSBY

HAMLET

HENRY V

THE ICEMAN COMETH

SAMSON AGONISTES

TWELFTH NIGHT

WALDEN

TWENTIETH CENTURY
INTERPRETATIONS
OF

THE SOUND
AND THE FURY

TWENTIETH CENTURY
INTERPRETATIONS
OF

THE SOUND
AND THE FURY

A Collection of Critical Essays

Edited by
MICHAEL H. COWAN

Prentice-Hall, Inc. *Englewood Cliffs, N. J.*

A SPECTRUM BOOK

Acknowledgments

The editor wishes to thank Random House, Inc. and Curtis Brown, Ltd. for permission to use excerpts from *The Sound and the Fury*. Copyright 1929 and renewed 1956 by William Faulkner. Copyright 1946 by Random House, Inc.

Contents

TWENTIETH CENTURY
INTERPRETATIONS
OF
THE SOUND
AND THE FURY

Introduction

by Michael H. Cowan

The Sound and the Fury, the fourth of William Faulkner's novels, was published in 1,789 copies on October 7, 1929, only two weeks before the Wall Street stock market crash signaled the onset of the most severe depression in American history—a crisis shared throughout the modern industrial world. The book went through two smaller printings in 1931, probably to capitalize on the notoriety of Faulkner's next novel, *Sanctuary*. This total of less than 3,300 copies sufficed his American publishers for over a decade. By the time the work was republished in 1946, it had been out of print for several years.[1]

Perhaps the book's lack of early popular success can be partly accounted for by the era of crisis into which it was thrust. Perhaps Faulkner's story of the fall of a small-town Southern family with aristocratic pretensions seemed perversely irrelevant to a nation trying to recover from a series of unprecedented economic and social blows—a nation that could derive only small consolation from Jason Compson's losses in cotton speculation and his diatribes against Eastern Jewish bankers. Perhaps the novel's complex and difficult technique irritated potential readers who were demanding a muscular gospel of political action and economic reform, not an intricate psychological analysis of a family in decay. Such social preoccupations, for example, seem to have dictated Lionel Trilling's dismissal of the book in 1931 as "essentially parochial."

Some early reviewers were even harsher in judgment. Noting that Faulkner had created a "nightmare group" of characters—a father turned cynic and alcoholic, the mother a demanding hypochondriac, their daughter cast out after bearing an illegitimate child, and their three sons an obsession-driven suicide, a bitter two-bit materialist, and a helpless idiot—certain critics concluded that the

---

[1] Publication information comes from James B. Meriwether, "Notes on the Textual History of *The Sound and the Fury*," *The Papers of the Bibliographical Society of America*, LVI (1962), 285-316.

young novelist was a decadent Southerner who enjoyed exploiting pathological material for its own sake. Such judgments seemed reinforced by the publication in 1931 of *Sanctuary,* which struck Henry Seidel Canby as belonging at the center of "the cult of cruelty." [2]

Most early critics, however, gave the book a much higher rating. One English reviewer argued that, "in conception and execution this novel has that kind of newness, and gives that shock to the imagination, which puts its author in the running for the highest stakes." [3] During the 1930's, when major French critics such as André Malraux, Maurice le Breton, and Jean-Paul Sartre were greeting Faulkner's novels with acclaim and shrewd analysis, Sartre published his influential essay on the theme of time in *The Sound and the Fury* and Maurice Coindreau translated the novel into French. With the appearance of the Modern Library edition in 1946, the novel was made available for the first time to a postwar generation of young American readers—a generation that was ready for it.[4] Since 1950 it has been translated into over half a dozen languages and has become, on the whole, Faulkner's most popular and most respected novel, a landmark in American and modern literary history.

This growth of the book's reputation has been based at least partly on the growing recognition that, in an oblique but profound way, *The Sound and the Fury* does have much to say about and to the age in which it appeared. By an appropriate coincidence, 1929 also witnessed the publication of Hemingway's *A Farewell to Arms* and Remarque's *All Quiet on the Western Front.* In reflecting a disenchantment with the first world war and with the postwar world, such books struck a mood that finds many echoes in Faulkner's novel. If we add to such a mood the striking experimental

[2] Lionel Trilling, "Mr. Faulkner's World," *The Nation,* CXXXIII (November 4, 1931), 491-92; Camille J. McCole, "The Nightmare Literature of William Faulkner," *Catholic World,* CXLI (August, 1935), 576-83; Henry Seidel Canby, "The School of Cruelty," *Saturday Review of Literature,* VII (March 21, 1931), 673-74.

[3] L. A. G. Strong in *The Spectator,* CXLVI (April 25, 1931), 674.

[4] There are actually two Modern Library editions of the novel. The 1946 version included both *The Sound and the Fury* and *As I Lay Dying* and printed as a "Foreword" the historical appendix on the Compsons that Faulkner had written originally for Malcolm Cowley's *Portable Faulkner,* which appeared in the same year. The more recent edition (also a Vintage book) prints *The Sound and the Fury* by itself, with the appendix in its proper place. My discussion uses the pagination of the newer edition, which reproduces photographically the 1929 edition.

qualities of his style, we can understand why the book finds an appropriate place in the line of major European works appearing after the war: Pound's first "Cantos" (1919), Eliot's "The Waste Land" (1922), Joyce's *Ulysses* (1922), Mann's *The Magic Mountain* (1924), and Kafka's *The Castle* (1926). Like Eliot's influential poem, Faulkner's poetic novel attempted—even in its techniques—to shore the fragments of such traditional values as love and dignity against the moral ruins of modern civilization and the modern consciousness.

To call *The Sound and the Fury* "modern," therefore, is not to deny its traditional qualities. An early reviewer claimed it was as "full of terror as a Greek tragedy," [5] and critics have been prompted to relate the disintegration of the Compsons to the tragedies of major families in Old Testament stories, in Greek and Shakespearean drama, and in nineteenth-century novels like *The Brothers Karamazov*. Figures like Maury Bascomb and names like Herbert Head and Gerald Bland might well suggest characters from Balzac and Dickens, two of Faulkner's favorite novelists. And the purple rhetoric of Quentin's self-indulging and melancholy reveries seems closely related to similar postures in Byron, Keats, Tennyson, and Swineburne, not to mention Joyce's Stephen Dedalus or Eliot's Prufrock.

Many other elements of the novel, however, point to roots in Faulkner's own regional and national soils. The banter and pranks of the Negro servant Luster are in the Southwestern tradition of folk humor that helped produce Mark Twain. The isolated characters in the novel have older cousins not only in Dickens' orphans and in Joyce's alienated individuals but in Melville's Ishmael and Twain's Huck Finn. The framework of Southern provincial life offers parallels both to European provincial novels and to American works by George Washington Cable, Sherwood Anderson, and Sinclair Lewis. And the gothic qualities of Faulkner's story suggest echoes of *The House of the Seven Gables,* Melville's *Pierre,* and the "grotesques" of *Winesburg, Ohio.* To mention such older European and American works is not to suggest specific literary sources for *The Sound and the Fury,* but simply to indicate the rich and complex cultural context out of which the book emerged and some grounds for its many-faceted appeal to the modern reader.

*　　　*　　　*

In October 1928, after typing the final version of *The Sound*

[5] Abbott Martin in *Sewanee Review,* XXXVIII (January, 1930), 115-16.

and the Fury in the New York apartment of his friend and literary agent Ben Wasson, Faulkner told Wasson, "Read this, Bud. It's a real sonofabitch." [6] The remark reflects the pride he felt in a novel that, he explained in 1931, "I had written my guts into."

Though he probably wrote most of the book during six months of intensive work in 1928, elements of it germinated for a much longer period. Faulkner never specified when he first began to think of a story based, as he variously put it, on his image of some children on the day of their grandmother's funeral or on "a mental picture . . . of the muddy seat of a little girl's drawers in a pear tree." [7] As early as 1925, however, he had described an idiot whose eyes "were clear and blue as cornflowers" and who "gripped tightly in one fist a narcissus." [8]

Though Faulkner described only vaguely and briefly the process by which he composed the novel, the manuscript shows that he revised it carefully before publication. His technique prompted Conrad Aiken, in 1939, to speak of the book as "a novelist's novel —a whole textbook on the craft of fiction in itself." [9] Written at the outset of the most productive period of his career, *The Sound and the Fury* marked the beginning of Faulkner's confidence in himself as a major professional writer. Perhaps this is one reason that it became for him, as he often said, "the book I feel tenderest towards."

This tenderness may also have had deeper autobiographical sources. Faulkner argued in 1957 that a novelist should tell "about people . . . out of his experience, his observation, and his imagination," and his memories of his own childhood and youth may have helped him obey these dicta in *The Sound and the Fury*. In the economic decline of his family from the days of his colorful great-grandfather, the sensitive young novelist (like Quentin Compson in this respect) may have sensed a problematic interaction of fate, history, and people that might be examined meditatively by creation of the Compson family. Himself the oldest of four brothers, Faulkner could imagine how the four Compson children might interact. His own grandmother, like the Compson children's, was called "Damuddy." The family's Negro nurse, "Mammy" Callie

[6] Quoted in Meriwether, "Textual History," p. 289.

[7] See the interviews included in this collection.

[8] "The Kingdom of God," in William Faulkner, *New Orleans Sketches*, with an introduction by Carvel Collins (New Brunswick, N. J.; Rutgers University Press, 1958), pp. 111-19.

[9] Conrad Aiken, "William Faulkner: The Novel as Form," *The Atlantic Monthly*, CLXIV (November, 1939), 650-54.

Barr, remained in Faulkner's employ until her death in 1940; and in dedicating *Go Down, Moses* (1942) to this woman "who was born in slavery and who gave to my family a fidelity without stint or calculation of recompense and to my childhood an immeasurable devotion and love," Faulkner was suggesting qualities that appear in the Compsons' servant Dilsey.[10]

Though such fragments of Faulkner's youth do not make *The Sound and the Fury* a covert autobiography, they do help account for part of its emotional strength. It may be significant that in no other novel did Faulkner deal so extensively with children. If *The Sound and the Fury* is most obviously the story of a family's decline and fall and, in its larger metaphorical implications, the picture of a fallen modern world, it is simultaneously the story of a fall that takes place in every generation—the loss (as well, perhaps, as gain) that comes with growing up. As Maxwell Geismar put it in 1942:

> Beneath the technical virtuosity of the novel, beneath the portrait of a decaying Southern landed aristocracy and the emergence of the modern industrial order . . . the theme of the novel is basically the disenchantment of an evil maturity. What we feel in 'The Sound and the Fury' is all the comfort and affection of a childhood world at the moment of its impact with adult values; at the moment of its realization of sin.[11]

If one of the novel's major themes is time—and certainly more critics have written on this theme than on any other aspect of it— it is time dramatized more specifically in the varying reactions of the Compson children to their individual and overlapping pasts —pasts often made more paradisal in the remembering than in the initial experiencing.

* * *

Because Faulkner presents so carefully the memories of the three Compson brothers—each trapped by the varying patterns of isolation that form another major theme in the novel—it is tempting to read the work as a document of literary naturalism and to take in a literal biological sense Faulkner's statement that he had originally intended to tell a story of "blood gone bad." Mr. Compson speaks for a naturalistic point of view within the novel when he insists to

[10] See James W. Webb and A. Wigfall Green, eds., *William Faulkner of Oxford* (Baton Rouge: Louisiana State University Press, 1965).

[11] Maxwell Geismar, *Writers in Crisis* (Boston: Houghton Mifflin Company, 1942), p. 158.

Quentin that "general truth" consists of "the sequence of natural events and their causes which shadows every mans brow" (p. 220) or that man is "the sum of his climatic experiences" (p. 153).

From this point of view, it is "natural" that a healthy woman like Caddy should want sexual experience—"Women are never virgins," says Mr. Compson. "Purity is a negative state and therefore contrary to nature" (p. 143). It is also "natural," in the light of his early psychological conditioning in the romanticized Southern "code" of chivalry, that Quentin should be obsessed with preserving his sister's virginity. It is "natural," too, that Mr. Compson, nagged by his wife and shaken by the birth of an idiot son, by the sexual activities of his daughter, and by the suicide of another son, should take to drink and adopt a rigid skepticism to defend himself against the violence done to his sensitive, loving nature, just as it is "natural" that the girl Quentin, growing up without father or mother and treated like a "bitch" by Jason, should fulfill his predictions. The strong sense of pathos—as distinct from tragedy—in many aspects of the novel comes from the suggestion of an environmental, biological, and psychological "doom" that controls the lives of characters who cannot help being what they are—individuals for whom "freedom" is an illusory hope or rationalization.

The decay of the Compson family, seen in this way, is part of a universal cyclical rhythm of rising and falling, birth and death, from which no natural object can escape. Whatever happiness nature may provide man—and we can think of Benjy's love of the smell of trees and rain—it also frustrates again and again even the noblest of men. When Dilsey opens her cabin door on Easter Sunday, dressed in her best church-going clothes, and discovers a gray, clammy drizzle, she can only lift her face "into the driving day with an expression at once fatalistic and of a child's astonished disappointment" (p. 331).

In its most pessimistic form, this naturalistic point of view is reflected in the novel's title, which Faulkner took from *Macbeth:*

> Out, out, brief candle!
> Life's but a walking shadow, a poor player
> That struts and frets his hour upon the stage,
> And then is heard no more. It is a tale
> Told by an idiot, full of sound and fury,
> Signifying nothing.

Though the title refers most obviously to Benjy's section, it also casts a dark light on many other aspects of the novel. All the brothers are, in varying ways, telling tales of sound and fury. Jason struts and frets through a day made unstable by the cotton market and his niece's sexual escapades. Quentin, plagued by his own and other shadows, plays out a despairing drama in the final hours before he extinguishes the candle of his life.

This pessimistic tone is also at times suggested by the other major series of literary allusions in the novel, those referring to the story of Christ's crucifixion and resurrection.[12] In dating three sections of the novel to correspond to the Friday, Saturday, and Sunday of Easter weekend, 1928, Faulkner is able to suggest a set of traditional values that stand in ironic contrast to the actual values held by many members of the Compson world. For several Compsons, in fact, traditional Christian rhetoric takes on new and perverted meanings as they use it for self-serving ends. In varying degrees, Quentin, Jason, and Mrs. Compson suggest a Calvinism gone morbid—an attitude differing from pessimistic naturalism only in that "doom" is defined not as the product of natural causes but as the will of a hard and inscrutable God, a jealous Old Testament Jehovah. Caroline Compson believes herself, like Job, the innocent victim of God's arbitrary assertion of power. She indulges in a travesty on Puritan typology when she renames her youngest son after the Old Testament Benjamin in order to fulfill her histrionic sense of a curse on the house of Compson and, especially, on herself—her "sin" being, she believes, merely that of marrying a Compson. Her insincere posturings of self-abasement before this "judgment" are as selfish as Jason's:

> "I know you blame me," Mrs. Compson said, "for letting them off to go to church today. . . . The darkies are having a special Easter service. I promised Dilsey two weeks ago that they could get off."
> "Which means we'll eat cold dinner," Jason said, "or none at all."
> "I know it's my fault," Mrs. Compson said. "I know you blame me."
> "For what?" Jason said. "You never resurrected Christ, did you."
> (p. 348)

Mrs. Compson's posturings reinforce symbiotically Jason's own exploitation of the role of innocent victim crucified by a cruel "Omnipotence" (p. 382). There is a similar masochistic egotism in Quentin's pathetic attempts to play Romantic versions of Christ and Satan—either to sacrifice or to damn himself for the glory of traditional values, as he narrowly interprets these values.

---

[12] Many essays in this collection deal generally with these allusions; for the most detailed discussion see the essay by Carvel Collins.

In the context of these perversions of traditional Christian meaning, Dilsey's more primitive and yet more mature Christian faith
assumes dramatic strength. She seems to recognize that, in one sense,
both nature and society are "fallen" worlds, subject to death, im-
perfection, and even sin. And yet her moral actions in the face of
this recognition imply a perspective that asserts a possibility beyond
either the naturalistic or negative Calvinistic interpretations of experience. Dilsey's faith places less stress on a remote and punishing
God than on a personal God whose divine love passes human understanding. This perspective, which reaches its climax in the Negro
preacher's Easter sermon, does not deny the natural limits and finite
suffering of man but suggests that, like Christ's crucifixion, such
experience has meaning beyond a self-pitying awareness of natural
death. By choosing to believe in a vision of life that stresses "de
resurrection en de light" rather than "de darkness en de death,"
Dilsey, in her sincere humility, becomes a symbol of individual
dignity and of the possibilities of human freedom.

In the complex interaction of the vision of "the sound and the
fury" with the vision of "de power en de glory" lie the many and
ambiguous tones of the novel—a twilight zone of light and shadow,
youth and decay, freedom and fate, hope and despair, that can
never be resolved by the rational mind of man or by the explicit
statement of Faulkner. For all that he implies about the causes or
meaning of experiences, Faulkner leaves a strong sense of mystery
as to the ultimate source of natural and human processes in the
novel. Dilsey has made this mystery the basis of her Christian faith
—a faith that shares many moral qualities with the humanist's tragic
optimism—but Faulkner himself refuses to reduce the complexities
of experience to a simple metaphysical assertion. One of the most
fascinating and frustrating aspects of *The Sound and the Fury,* in
fact, is its ultimate ambiguity. Like much of the greatest modern
literature, it is a novel of implication rather than of explanation,
of concrete dramatization rather than of abstract analysis.

*   *   *

Our understanding of Faulkner's major stylistic and structural
techniques, therefore, is crucial to our full appreciation of the
novel's implied meanings. As critics have pointed out, one of his
most important techniques is his use of symbolic actions and
juxtapositions. Faulkner often uses juxtaposition for ironic effect.
Jason can in one breath defend and in the next breath damn the
"redneck" farmers around Jefferson, or can chase wildly after his

niece at the same time that he proclaims his indifference to what she does. Caroline Compson can whine about her "burdens" while we watch Dilsey carry the real weight of the family's responsibilities.

Faulkner's most striking use of this technique, however, comes in the first two sections of the novel. By allowing the "streams of consciousness" of Benjy and Quentin to arrange data by association rather than by external chronology, he is able to create a compressed series of juxtapositions that both reveal the characteristics of the minds in which they occur and suggest the larger themes of the novel.[13] By interspersing Benjy's memories of Caddy's wedding (pp. 23-47) with his memories of four deaths (Damuddy's, Quentin's, Mr. Compson's, and Roskus'), Faulkner can suggest, among other things, the common denominator of loss in all five events. By interlocking Quentin's affair with the little Italian girl and his memories of childhood affairs with Caddy, or his ride with Gerald Bland and his memories of Dalton Ames, Faulkner suggests not only Quentin's obsessions and blind spots but a world outside the Compson family that may share many of that family's dilemmas. Just as impressionist painters create the tone of a painting by applying discrete or overlapping dots or slashes of paint, whose effect comes in the juxtaposition and interaction of such strokes in the eye of the observer, so Faulkner uses strokes of prose—a dab of one scene against the dab of another, slashes of different time levels overlapping into each other—in order to create a total "impression" that goes beyond the literal content of the individual strokes.

Equally a measure of Faulkner's stylistic skill is his use of figurative language in the novel. Each of the three Compson brothers, for example, narrates his section in a style appropriate not only to his character but to the themes of the whole book. Aside from his verbatim recording of others' words, Benjy speaks in simple sentences and in a simple diction that contains almost no similes or metaphors. Such remarks as "Caddy smelled like trees," however, do acquire larger meaning for the reader. Jason's sentences are for the most part both informal and aphoristic ("Once a bitch, always a bitch"), and his language indulges in slang, colloquial similes ("her face looked like she had polished it with a gun rag," "we went past her like a fire engine"), and sarcastic understatement or hyperbole ("six niggers that cant even stand up out of a chair unless they've got a pan full of bread and meat to balance them," "they can bring all Beale Street and all bedlam in here and two of them

[13] See especially the essays by Irving Howe, Olga Vickery, and John Hunt in this collection.

can sleep in my bed and another one can have my place at the table too"). Such language reveals a clever and vital mind caught in the prejudices of his day and the conventions of a bitter and narrow materialism.

The style of Quentin's section is decidedly more complex than that of his brothers' sections; and if such a style is appropriate to his level of intelligence and education and to his emotional pre-occupations, it has also made his section the most difficult to understand. Quentin's mind shifts not only more frequently than Benjy's (almost 200 times as compared to about 100 time shifts in Benjy's section) but often thinks in sentence fragments—a reflection of the frenetic mental pace belied by his deliberate external actions on June 2. Whereas Benjy almost never repeats himself in memory (a useful strategy through which Faulkner can suggest Benjy's pre-occupations and, at the same time, present as much "objective" information as possible), Quentin obsessively repeats key scenes and, especially, phrases from his past: "the voice that breathed o'er Eden," Dalton Ames, Dalton Ames, Dalton Ames," "one minute she was standing there," "Father I have committed."

In such repetitions, occurring often in differing contexts, Faulkner suggests the way in which Quentin is fusing widely varying experiences to conform to the rigid pattern of his obsessions. A good example of this fusing is the often repeated question, "Did you ever have a sister?" and its counterpart, the dangling phrase, "who never had a sister." In the course of Quentin's narrative, he uses these phrases to test many males of his actual and his literary experience: his father, Dalton Ames, Gerald Bland, Shreve, Hamlet, St. Francis, and even Jesus. In each case, Quentin distorts both the actual and the literary figures into conformity with his attempt to see himself as a Romantic hero, defier of fate, sacrificial redeemer of damned experience.

The same fusing tendencies can be seen in Quentin's reactions to his literal experiences on June 2. Such experiences become characteristically the basis for similes and metaphors that reveal his ultimate concerns. An excellent example is a passage (p. 149) in which Quentin leaves a bridge from which three boys have been trying vainly to catch a gigantic trout:

> "Cant anybody catch that fish," the first said. They leaned on the rail, looking down into the water, the three poles like three slanting threads of yellow fire in the sun. I walked upon my shadow, tramping it into the dappled shade of trees again. The road curved, mounting away from the water. It crossed the hill, then descended

winding, carrying the eye, the mind on ahead beneath a still green
tunnel, and the square cupola above the trees and the round eye
of the clock but far enough. I sat down at the roadside. The grass was
ankle deep, myriad. The shadows on the road were as still as if they
had been put there with a stencil, with slanting pencils of sunlight.
But it was only a train, and after a while it died away beyond the
trees, the long sound, and then I could hear my watch and the train
dying away, as though it were running through another month or
another summer somewhere, rushing away under the poised gull and
all things rushing. Except Gerald. He would be sort of grand too,
pulling in lonely state across the noon, rowing himself right out of
noon, up the long bright air like an apotheosis, mounting into a
drowsing infinity where only he and the gull, the one terrifically
motionless, the other in a steady and measured pull and recover
that partook of inertia itself, the world punily beneath their shadows
on the sun. Caddy that blackguard that blackguard Caddy

Though the passage contains gaps in objective information more
characteristic of a mind thinking to itself than of one communicat-
ing to others (e.g., the jump from "pencils of sunlight" to "But it
was only a train"), it does suggest an overall progression. It begins
with a series of concrete descriptions—poles in the water, the sun
overhead, the shadows of Quentin and trees on the road, the clock
in the Unitarian steeple, the sound of a train in the distance. But
Quentin cannot keep his mind on the literality of these sensations.
Through a cumulative elaboration of their metaphorical possibilities, Quentin almost instinctively interweaves them into the fabric
of his basic concerns. He compares the poles to "slanting threads of
yellow fire in the sun," and such threads then become the "slanting
pencils of sunlight" that have drawn both the trees' and Quentin's
shadows. His eye is carried to the "round eye of the clock" on the
church steeple, and this socially and religiously suggestive eye of
time is then linked with its natural neighbor above the treetops,
the sun, the universal timekeeper whose light paradoxically creates
shadows. These time-created shadows become associated with the
"green tunnel" down which Quentin looks and with the "dying"
sound of the train, and the train begins to travel into Quentin's
past, "as though it were running through another month or another
summer somewhere." [14] Concurrently, there is a movement from the
fish in the water upward (via the mounting road and the Unitarian

[14] Cf. the "long corridor of grey halflight where all stable things had become
shadowy paradoxical all I had done shadows all I had felt suffered taking visible
form inherent themselves with the denial of the significance they should have
affirmed" (p. 211).

church steeple) toward a sky that becomes a metaphorical river in which Gerald Bland and the gull cast "their shadows on the sun" —fish, gull, water, shadows, sun, clock, Gerald, and finally Dalton Ames ("that blackguard") blending into an "apotheosis" that is the symbolic object of Quentin's hatred and of his jealous longing: an eternal (and perhaps unattainable) state beyond the finite suffering and dying of the "puny" world in which Quentin is trapped.

*   *   *

The cumulative thematic implications that come from linking specific images by means of juxtaposition, repetition, and implied association or contrast appear in their most concentrated form in Quentin's section. Faulkner uses the same techniques less obviously, however, to reinforce the structure of the entire novel. Most of the symbols in *The Sound and the Fury* begin as literal referents to physical or psychological reality. When water first appears in Benjy's section, it is literally water; shadows are literally shadows; flowers, rain, and trees, dirt and mud, fire and sunlight, mirrors and slippers, money and golf balls all appear to Benjy as actual phenomena. The metaphorical resonances of these and other key words and images do not begin to appear until we have struggled a good way into his section, and such resonances do not acquire their full range of implication until we experience new contexts for these words and images in the remaining sections of the novel. Guided by Faulkner, the reader must move gradually from concrete experiences to complex implications, from confusion to tentative understanding.

In total effect, the novel's images symbolize no simple meaning for the Compson world. If fire gives pleasure to Benjy, it also burns him; if it suggests destruction to Quentin, it also suggests a vision of eternity beyond destruction. If shadows link characters to an earthy world of animal instincts and physical limits, they also point to a home for imaginations and souls. If water and flowers become associated with purity, happiness, creativity, and love, they also take on overtones of impurity, narcissism, pain, and death. Such ambiguous images do not solve experience, but add to its rich complexity.

Even in the final section of the novel, Faulkner refrains from explicit meditation (at least, in his own voice) on the ultimate meaning of the novel. More important and moving than any obvious symbols in this section are its concrete physical pictures. In keeping with the "objective" narrative of the section by an "outsider," figurative language is sparse.[15] Dilsey's frame is (with thematic appropriateness) "like a ruin or a landmark," jaybirds whirl in the wind "like gaudy scraps of cloth or paper," Dilsey clutches Mrs. Compson's water bottle "by the neck like a dead hen," and as she works she begins to sing louder "as if her voice too had been thawed out by the growing warmth." Neither elaborate nor surprising, such similes suggest both Dilsey's realistic perspective on the Compson world and Faulkner's cautious appraisal of that world.

Faulkner liked to stress in interviews that, even in the fourth section, he had "failed" to explore the full meaning of the Compsons' fall. But such failure was also a measure to him of the book's vitality. As he told Malcolm Cowley, in defending the inconsistencies between the novel and the 1946 appendix, "the book is still alive after 15 years, and being still alive is growing, changing . . . ." [16] By dramatizing this openness to changing experience, even when shadowed by pathos and tragedy, *The Sound and the Fury* remains a challenge and a joy to the careful modern reader.

*   *   *

I have selected the following essays from a huge body of criticism on *The Sound and the Fury*, much of it repetitious. No doubt, long-time students of the novel will find a favorite essay or two missing. I have chosen not to reprint here the three essays readily available in Robert Penn Warren's Twentieth Century Views collection on Faulkner. I regret having to condense severely many of the essays and can only plead the limitations of space. Page references are to the 1946 Modern Library edition of the novel, with the exception of the introduction, appendix, and essay by Hunt, which use the more recent Modern Library and Vintage edition.

[15] A thematically appropriate exception to this sparseness is the Negro church service, in which Faulkner pushes language toward paradox. See the essay by Walter Slatoff in this collection.
[16] Quoted in Malcolm Cowley, *The Faulkner-Cowley File: Letters and Memories, 1944-1962* (New York: Random House, Inc., 1966), pp. 89-90.

Faulkner Discusses *The Sound and the Fury*

Remarks in Japan, 1955

In my own estimation, none of [my stories] are good enough, that's why I have spent thirty years writing another one, hoping that one would be good enough. And so my personal feeling would be a tenderness for the one which caused me the most anguish, just as the mother might feel for the child, and the one that caused me the most anguish and is to me the finest failure is *The Sound and the Fury*. That's the one that I feel most tender toward. . . .

That began as a short story, it was a story without plot, of some children being sent away from the house during the grandmother's funeral. They were too young to be told what was going on and they saw things only incidentally to the childish games they were playing, which was the lugubrious matter of removing the corpse from the house, etc., and then the idea struck me to see how much more I could have got out of the idea of the blind self-centeredness of innocence, typified by children, if one of those children had been truly innocent, that is, an idiot. So the idiot was born and then I became interested in the relationship of the idiot to the world that he was in but would never be able to cope with and just where could he get the tenderness, the help, to shield him in his innocence. I mean 'innocence' in the sense that God had stricken him blind at birth, that is, mindless at birth, there was nothing he could ever do about it. And so the character of his sister began to emerge, then the brother, who, that Jason (who to me represented complete evil. He's the most vicious character in my opinion I ever thought of), then he appeared. By that time I found out I couldn't possibly tell that in a short story. And so I told the idiot's experience of that day, and that was incomprehensible, even I could not have told what was going on then, so I had to write another chapter. Then I decided to let Quentin tell his version of that same day, or that

From Faulkner at Nagano, *ed. Robert A. Jelliffe. (Tokyo Kenkyusha Ltd., 1956), pp. 102-6. Reprinted by permission of the publisher. Copyright © 1956 by Kenkyusha Ltd.*

same occasion, so he told it. Then there had to be the counterpoint, which was the other brother, Jason. By that time it was completely confusing. I knew that it was not anywhere near finished and then I had to write another section from the outside with an outsider, which was the writer, to tell what had happened on that particular day. And that's how that book grew. That is, I wrote that same story four times. None of them were right, but I had anguished so much that I could not throw any of it away and start over, so I printed it in the four sections. . . .

One time I thought of printing that first section in different colors, but that would have been too expensive. . . . But if it could have been printed in different colors . . . anyone reading it could keep up with who was talking and who was thinking this and what time, what moment in time, it was. To that idiot, time was not a continuation, it was an instant, there was no yesterday and no tomorrow, it all is this moment, it all is [now] to him. He cannot distinguish between what was last year and what will be tomorrow, he doesn't know whether he dreamed it, or saw it.

Interview with Cynthia Grenier, 1955

The book which took the most agony was *The Sound and the Fury*. Took me five years of re-working and re-writing. Never did finish it. . . . It started out as a short story about two children being sent out to play in the yard during their grandmother's funeral. Only one of the little girls was big enough to climb a tree to look in the window to see what was going on. It was going to be a story of blood gone bad. The story told wasn't all. The idiot child had started out as a simple prop at first as a bid for extra sympathy. Then I thought what would the story be told like as he saw it. So I had him look at it. When I'd finished I had a quarter of the book written, but it still wasn't all. It still wasn't enough. So then Quentin told the story as he saw it and it still wasn't enough. Then Jason told the story and it still wasn't enough. Then I tried to tell the story and it still wasn't enough, and so I wrote the appendix and it wasn't enough. It's the book I feel tenderest towards. I couldn't leave it alone, and I never could tell it right,

---

"The Art of Fiction: An Interview with William Faulkner—September, 1955," by *Cynthia Grenier. From* Accent, *XVI (Summer, 1956), 172-73. Copyright, 1956, by* Accent.

though I tried hard and would like to try again though I'd probably fail again. It's the tragedy of two lost women: Caddy and her daughter.

Interview with Jean Stein, 1956

FAULKNER: Since none of my work has met my own standards, I must judge it on the basis of that one which caused me the most grief and anguish, as the mother loves the child who became the thief or murderer more than the one who became the priest.

INTERVIEWER: What work is that?

FAULKNER: *The Sound and the Fury.* I wrote it five separate times, trying to tell the story, to rid myself of the dream which would continue to anguish me until I did. It's a tragedy of two lost women: Caddy and her daughter. Dilsey is one of my own favorite characters, because she is brave, courageous, generous, gentle, and honest. She's much more brave and honest and generous than me.

INTERVIEWER: How did *The Sound and the Fury* begin?

FAULKNER: It began with a mental picture. I didn't realize at the time it was symbolical. The picture was of the muddy seat of a little girl's drawers in a pear tree, where she could see through a window where her grandmother's funeral was taking place and report what was happening to her brothers on the ground below. By the time I explained who they were and what they were doing and how her pants got muddy, I realized it would be impossible to get all of it into a short story and that it would have to be a book. And then I realized the symbolism of the soiled pants, and that image was replaced by one of the fatherless and motherless girl climbing down the rainpipe to escape from the only home she had, where she had never been offered love or affection or understanding.

I had already begun to tell the story through the eyes of the idiot child, since I felt that it would be more effective as told by someone capable only of knowing what happened, but not why. I saw that I had not told the story that time. I tried to tell it again, the

From "An Interview with William Faulkner," by Jean Stein. From Writers at Work: The Paris Review Interviews, *1st Series, ed. Malcolm Cowley (New York: The Viking Press, Inc., 1959; London: Martin Secker and Warburg, Ltd., 1959), pp. 130-32. All Rights Reserved. First published in* The Paris Review, *XII (Spring, 1956). Reprinted with permission from the author,* The Paris Review, The Viking Press, Inc., *and Martin Secker and Warburg, Ltd.*

same story through the eyes of another brother. That was still not it. I told it for the third time through the eyes of the third brother. That was still not it. I tried to gather the pieces together and fill in the gaps by making myself the spokesman. It was still not complete, not until fifteen years after the book was published, when I wrote as an appendix to another book the final effort to get the story told and off my mind, so that I myself could have some peace from it. . . .

INTERVIEWER: What emotion does Benjy arouse in you?

FAULKNER: The only emotion I can have for Benjy is grief and pity for all mankind. You can't feel anything for Benjy because he doesn't feel anything. The only thing I can feel about him personally is concern as to whether he is believable as I created him. He was a prologue, like the gravedigger in the Elizabethan dramas. He serves his purpose and is gone. Benjy is incapable of good and evil because he had no knowledge of good and evil.

INTERVIEWER: Could Benjy feel love?

FAULKNER: Benjy wasn't rational enough even to be selfish. He was an animal. He recognized tenderness and love though he could not have named them, and it was the threat to tenderness and love that caused him to bellow when he felt the change in Caddy. He no longer had Caddy; being an idiot he was not even aware that Caddy was missing. He knew only that something was wrong, which left a vacuum in which he grieved. He tried to fill that vacuum. The only thing he had was one of Caddy's discarded slippers. The slipper was his tenderness and love which he could not have named, but he knew only that it was missing. He was dirty because he couldn't coordinate and because dirt meant nothing to him. He could no more distinguish between dirt and cleanliness than between good and evil. The slipper gave him comfort even though he no longer remembered the person to whom it had once belonged, any more than he could remember why he grieved. If Caddy had reappeared he probably would not have known her.

INTERVIEWER: Does the narcissus given to Benjy have some significance?

FAULKNER: The narcissus was given to Benjy to distract his attention. It was simply a flower which happened to be handy that fifth of April. It was not deliberate.

Discussions at the University of Virginia, 1957-58

Q. Mr. Faulkner, in *The Sound and the Fury* the first three sections of that book are narrated by one of the four Compson children, and in view of the fact that Caddy figures so prominently, is there any particular reason why you didn't have a section . . . giving her views or impressions of what went on?

A. That's a good question. That—the explanation of that whole book is in that. It began with the picture of the little girl's muddy drawers, climbing that tree to look in the parlor window with her brothers that didn't have the courage to climb the tree waiting to see what she saw. And I tried first to tell it with one brother, and that wasn't enough. That was Section One. I tried with another brother, and that wasn't enough. That was Section Two. I tried the third brother, because Caddy was still to me too beautiful and too moving to reduce her to telling what was going on, that it would be more passionate to see her through somebody else's eyes, I thought. And that failed and I tried myself—the fourth section—to tell what happened, and I still failed. . . .

Q. Mr. Faulkner, I am interested in the symbolism in *The Sound and the Fury,* and I wasn't able to figure exactly the significance of the shadow symbol in Quentin. It's referred to over and over again: he steps in the shadow, shadow is before him, the shadow is often after him. Well then, what is the significance of his shadow?

A. That wasn't a deliberate symbolism. I would say that that shadow that stayed on his mind so much was foreknowledge of his own death, that he was— Death is here, shall I step into it, or shall I step away from it a little longer? I won't escape it, but shall I accept it now or shall I put it off until next Friday. I think that if it had any reason that must have been it. . . .

Q. Mr. Faulkner, I'd like to ask you about Quentin and his relationship with his father. I think many readers get the impression that Quentin is the way he is to a large extent because of his father's lack of values, or the fact that he doesn't seem to pass down to his son many values that will sustain him. Do you think that Quentin winds up the way he does primarily because of that, or

Excerpted from Faulkner in the University, *ed. Frederick L. Gwynn and Joseph L. Blotner (Charlottesville: University of Virginia Press, 1959). Copyright © 1959 by the University of Virginia Press. Reprinted with permission of the publisher.*

are we meant to see, would you say, that the action . . . comes primarily from what he is, abetted by what he gets from his father?

A. The action as portrayed by Quentin was transmitted to him through his father. There was a basic failure before that. The grandfather had been a failed brigadier twice in the Civil War. It was the—the basic failure Quentin inherited through his father, or beyond his father. It was a—something had happened somewhere between the first Compson and Quentin. The first Compson was a bold ruthless man who came into Mississippi as a free forester to grasp where and when he could and wanted to, and established what should have been a princely line, and that princely line decayed. . . .

Q. Mr. Faulkner, in your speech at Stockholm you expressed great faith in mankind . . . not only to endure but prevail. . . . Do you think that's the impression the average reader would get after reading *The Sound and the Fury?*

A. I can't answer that because I don't know what the average reader gets from reading the book. . . . But in my opinion, yes, that is what I was talking about in all the books, and I failed to say it. I agree with you, I did fail. But that was what I was trying to say—that man will prevail, will endure because he is capable of compassion and honor and pride and endurance. . . .

Q. Mr. Faulkner, when you say man has prevailed do you mean individual man has prevailed or group man?

A. Man as a part of life.

Q. . . . Quentin, for instance, . . . seemed to have the cards stacked against him. . . .

A. True, and his mother wasn't much good and he had an idiot brother, and yet in that whole family there was Dilsey that held the whole thing together and would continue to hold the whole thing together for no reward, that the will of man to prevail will even take the nether channel of the black man, black race, before it will relinquish, succumb, be defeated. . . .

[Q. In connection with the character of Christ, did you make any conscious attempts in *The Sound and the Fury* to use Christian references, as a number of critics have suggested?

A. No. I was just trying to tell a story of Caddy, the little girl who had muddied her drawers and was climbing up to look in the window where her grandmother lay dead.

Q. But Benjy, for example, is thirty-three years old, the traditional age of Christ at death.

A. Yes. That was a ready-made axe to use, but it was just one of several tools. . . .

Q. Your work has sometimes been compared with that of Hawthorne's tales with hard-hearted people like Jason. Do you think that one of the things that's wrong with the South is that there are too many characters like this, like Jason Compson, in it?

A. Yes, there are too many Jasons in the South who can be successful, just as there are too many Quentins in the South who are too sensitive to face its reality. . . .

Q. In *The Sound and the Fury,* where Quentin sees the boys fishing, does his remark about the big fish have any symbolism? He says to them, I hope you don't catch that big fish, he deserves to be let alone.

A. Well, it doesn't have any meaning by itself, but Quentin knows he is going to die and he sees things much more clearly than he would otherwise. He sees things that are more important to him since he doesn't have to worry about them now, and when he wants the old fish to live, it may represent his unconscious desire for endurance, both for himself and for his people. It is just like when some people know they are going to die, and the dross is burned away and they know they can say things because in a while they won't be around to have to defend them.

Q. In the last part of Quentin's section, why do you begin to omit capitals on the names and on "I"?

A. Because Quentin is a dying man, he is already out of life, and those things that were important in life don't mean anything to him any more. . . .

Q. What is the trouble with the Compsons?

A. They are still living in the attitudes of 1859 or '60.

Q. Why is it that Mrs. Compson refers to Benjy as having been sold into Egypt? Wasn't that Joseph in the Bible? Is the mistake yours or hers?

A. Is there anybody who knows the Bible here?

Q. I looked it up and Benjamin was held hostage for Joseph.

A. Yes, that's why I used them interchangeably. . . .] *

Q. You had said previously that *The Sound and the Fury* came from the impression of a little girl up in a tree, and I wondered how you built it from that, and whether you just, as you said, let the story develop itself?

A. Well, impression is the wrong word. It's more an image, a

---

* The material within brackets was reconstructed from memory by Gwynn and Blotner after a failure in their recording equipment.

very moving image to me was of the children. 'Course, we didn't know at the time that one was an idiot, but they were three boys, one was a girl and the girl was the only one that was brave enough to climb that tree to look in the forbidden window to see what was going on. And . . . it took the rest of the four hundred pages to explain why she was brave enough to climb the tree to look in the window. It was an image, a picture to me, a very moving one, which was symbolized by the muddy bottom of her drawers as her brothers looked up into the apple tree that she had climbed to look in the window. And the symbolism of the muddy bottom of the drawers became the lost Caddy, which had caused one brother to commit suicide and the other brother had misused her money that she'd send back to the child, the daughter. . . .

Q. What is your purpose in writing into the first section of *The Sound and the Fury* passages that seem disjointed in themselves if the [ideas are] connected with one another?

A. . . . It seemed to me that the book approached nearer the dream if the groundwork of it was laid by the idiot, who was incapable of relevancy. . . . I shifted those sections back and forth to see where they went best, but my final decision was that . . . that was the best to do it, that was simply the groundwork of that story, as that idiot child saw it. He himself didn't know what he was seeing. That the only thing that held him into any sort of reality, into the world at all, was the trust that he had for his sister, that he knew that she loved him and would defend him, and so she was the whole world to him, and these things were flashes that were reflected on her as in a mirror. He didn't know what they meant. . . .

Q. What symbolic meaning did you give to the dates of *The Sound and the Fury?*

A. Now there's a matter of hunting around in the carpenter's shop to find a tool that will make a better chicken-house. And probably—I'm sure it was quite instinctive that I picked out Easter, that I wasn't writing any symbolism of the Passion Week at all. I just—that was a tool that was good for the particular corner I was going to turn in my chicken-house and so I used it. . . .

Q. . . . In *The Sound and the Fury* was Jason Compson . . . a bastard?

A. No. Not an actual one—only in behavior. . . .

Q. . . . May I ask if all of these characters in *The Sound and the Fury*—that you would call them "good people"?

A. I would call them tragic people. The good people, Dilsey,

the Negro woman, she was a good human being. That she held
that family together for not the hope of reward but just because it
was the decent and proper thing to do. . . .

Q. Mr. Faulkner, in reference to *The Sound and the Fury* again
is the "tale told by an idiot, full of sound and fury, signifying
nothing" applicable to Benjy as is generally thought, or perhaps
to Jason?

A. The title, of course, came from the first section, which was
Benjy. I thought the story was told in Benjy's section, and the
title came there. So it—in that sense it does apply to Benjy rather
than to anybody else, though the more I had to work on the book,
the more elastic the title became, until it covered the whole
family. . . .

Q. Mr. Faulkner, in *The Sound and the Fury,* can you tell me
exactly why some of that is written in italics? What does that de-
note?

A. I had to use some method to indicate to the reader that the
idiot had no sense of time. That what happened to him ten years
ago was just yesterday. The way I wanted to do it was to use different colored inks, but that would have cost so much, the publisher
couldn't undertake it.

Q. Doesn't that go on with Quentin, too?

A. Yes, because he was about half way between madness and
sanity. It wasn't as much as in Benjy's part, because Quentin was
only half way between Benjy and Jason. Jason didn't need italics
because he was quite sane.

Q. And another thing I notice, you don't advise that people have
to have a subject and predicate for verbs and all those things.

A. Well, that—I think that's really not a fair question. I was
trying to tell this story as it seemed to me that idiot child saw it.
And that idiot child to me didn't know what a quesion, what an
interrogation was. He didn't know too much about grammar, he
spoke only through his senses.

Q. I'm referring mostly to Quentin and he certainly—he attended
Harvard, he should have known.

A. Well, Quentin was an educated half-madman, and so he
dispensed with grammar. Because it was all clear to his half-mad
brain and it seemed to him it would be clear to anybody else's brain,
that what he saw was quite logical, quite clear. . . .

Q. Mr. Faulkner, I saw something not long ago that took *The
Sound and Fury* in four sections and tried to draw a parallel between the id, the ego, and super-ego and the author's person. Now

don't you think that is indicative of what a lot of critics and scholars
are doing today with the views of contemporary writers, making
psychological inferences and finding symbols which the author
never intended?

A. Well, I would say that the author didn't deliberately intend
but I think that in the same culture the background of the critic
and of the writer are so similar that a part of each one's history is
the seed which can be translated into the symbols which are
standardized within that culture. That is, the writer don't have to
know Freud to have written things which anyone who does know
Freud can divine and reduce to symbols. . . . But I think the
writer is primarily concerned in telling about people, in the only
terms he knows, which is out of his experience, his observation, and
his imagination. . . .

Q. Does it give the author as much pain as it does the reader to
produce scenes such as when Caddy wanted to see her baby and
Jason just drove by?

A. Yes, it does, but that's—the writer is not simply dragging that
in to pull a few tears, he is—he puts that down as an instance of
man's injustice to man. That man will always be unjust to man, yet
there must always be people, men and women who are capable of
the compassion toward that injustice and the hatred to that injustice, and the will to risk public opprobrium, to stand up and
say, That is rotten, this stinks, I won't have it. . . .

Q. Did Quentin before actually have that conversation with his
father about sleeping with his sister, or was that part of his—?

A. He never did. He said, If I were brave, I would—I might say
this to my father, whether it was a lie or not, or if I were—if I
would say this to my father, maybe he would answer me back the
magic word which would relieve me of this anguish and agony
which I live with. No, they were imaginary. He just said, Suppose
I say this to my father, would it help me, would it clarify, would
I see clearer what it is that I anguish over? *

Q. The feeling between him and his sister is pretty strong though,
isn't it?

* This is a good example of a Faulkner answer that students should treat with
skepticism. Most critics agree that internal evidence (see pp. 219-20 of the novel)
seems to indicate that Quentin actually did have the conversation with his father.
Since Faulkner gave this interview nearly twenty years after he wrote the novel—
and since he claimed he had not reread it—it is understandable that he could
misremember many actual details about the book. Another example is the question of whether the girl Quentin climbed down a drainpipe or a tree in order to
escape from the Compson house.

A. Yes, yes. But in Caddy's opinion he was such a weakling that even if they had been no kin, she would never have chosen him for her sweetheart. She would have chosen one like the ex-soldier she did. But never anybody like Quentin. . . .

Q. Mr. Faulkner, I'm curious about Jason. . . . That Negro boy tells him to keep his hands out of his pockets, because he's falling on his face all the time, he stumbles. Why, was he fat and clumsy . . . ?

A. Probably. That was a mannerism, keeping his hands in his pockets, to me that presaged his future, something of greediness and grasping, selfishness. That he may have kept his hands in his pocket to guard whatever colored rock that he had found that was to him, represented the million dollars he would like to have some day.

On William Faulkner's
The Sound and the Fury

by Evelyn Scott

I want to write something about *The Sound and the Fury* before
the fanfare in print can greet even the ears of the author. There
will be many, I am sure, who, without this assistance, will make
the discovery of the book as an important contribution to the
permanent literature of fiction. I shall be pleased, however, if some
others, lacking the opportunity for investigating individually the
hundred claims to greatness which America makes every year in the
name of art, may be led, through these comments, to a perusal
of this unique and distinguished novel. The publishers, who are
so much to be congratulated for presenting a little known writer
with the dignity of recognition which his talent deserves, call this
book "overwhelmingly powerful and even monstrous." Powerful
it is; and it may even be described as "monstrous" in all its implications of tragedy; but such tragedy has a noble essence.

The question has been put by a contemporary critic, a genuine
philosopher reviewing the arts, as to whether there exists for this
age of disillusion with religion, dedication to the objective program
of scientific inventiveness and general rejection of the teleology
which placed man emotionally at the center of his universe, the
spirit of which great tragedy is the expression. *The Sound and the
Fury* seems to me to offer a reply. Indeed I feel that however so-
phistical the argument of theology, man remains, in his heart, in
that important position. What he seeks now is a fresh justification
for the presumption of his emotions; and his present tragedy is
in a realization of the futility, up to date, of his search for another,
intellectually appropriate embodiment of the god that lives on,
however contradicated by "reason."

William Faulkner, the author of this tragedy, which has all the
spacious proportions of Greek art, may not consider his book in the

least expressive of the general dilemma to which I refer, but that quality in his writings which the emotionally timid will call "morbid," seems to be reflected from the impression, made on a sensitive and normally egoistic nature, of what is in the air. Too proud to solve the human problem evasively through any of the sleight-of-hand of puerile surface optimism, he embraces, to represent life, figures that do indeed symbolize a kind of despair; but not the despair that depresses or frustrates. His pessimism as to fact, and his acceptance of all the morally inimical possibilities of human nature, is unwavering. The result is, nonetheless, the reassertion of humanity in defeat that is, in the subjective sense, a triumph. This is no Pyrrhic victory made in debate with those powers of intelligence that may be used to destroy. It is the conquest of nature by art. Or rather, the refutation, by means of a work of art, of the belittling of the materialists; and the work itself is in that category of facts which popular scientific thinking has made an ultimate. Here is beauty sprung from the perfect *realization* of what a more limiting morality would describe as ugliness. Here is a humanity stripped of most of what was claimed for it by the Victorians, and the spectacle is moving as no sugar-coated drama ever could be. The result for the reader, if he is like myself, is an exaltation of faith in mankind. It is faith without, as yet, an argument; but it is the same faith which has always lived in the most ultimate expression of human spirit.

The Sound and the Fury is the story of the fall of a house, the collapse of a provincial aristocracy in a final debacle of insanity, recklessness, psychological perversion. The method of presentation is, as far as I know, unique. Book I is a statement of the tragedy as seen through the eyes of a thirty-three-year-old idiot son of the house, Benjy. Benjy is beautiful, as beautiful as one of the helpless angels, and the more so for the slightly repellent earthiness that is his. He is a better idiot than Dostoyevsky's because his simplicity is more convincingly united with the basic animal simplicity of creatures untried by the standards of a conscious and calculating humanity. It is as if, indeed, Blake's Tiger had been framed before us by the same Hand that made the Lamb, and, in opposition to Blake's conception, endowed with the same soul. Innocence is terrible as well as pathetic—and Benjy is terrible, sometimes terrifying. He is a Christ symbol, yet not, even in the way of the old orthodoxies, Christly. A Jesus asks for a conviction of sin and a confession before redemption. He acknowledges this as in his own history, tempting by the Devil the prelude to his renunciation. In every subtle sense, sin is the desire to sin, the awareness of sin, an assertion in innuendo that, by the very statement of virtue, sin *is*. Benjy is no saint with a wounded ego his own gesture can console. He is not anything—nothing with a name. He is alive. He can suffer. The simplicity of his suffering, the absence, for him, of any compensating sense of drama, leave him as naked of self-flattery as was the first man. Benjy is like Adam, with all he remembers in the garden and one foot in hell on earth. This was where knowledge began, and for Benjy time is too early for any spurious profiting by knowledge. It is a little as if the story of Hans Anderson's Little Mermaid had been taken away from the nursery and sentiment and made rather diabolically to grow up. Here is the Little Mermaid on the way to find her soul in an uncouth and incontinent body—but there is no happy ending. Benjy, born male and made neuter, doesn't want a soul. It is being thrust upon him, but only like a horrid bauble which he does not recognize. He holds in his hands—in his heart, exposed to the reader—something frightening, unnamed—*pain!* Benjy lives deeply in the senses. For the remainder of what he sees as life, he lives as crudely as in allegory, vicariously, through uncritical perception of his adored sister (she smells to him like "leaves") and, in such emotional absolutism, traces for us her broken marriage, her departure forever from an unlovely home, her return by proxy in the person of her illegitimate daughter, Quentin, who, for Benjy, takes the mother's place.

Book II of the novel deals with another—the original Quentin, for whom the baby girl of later events is named. This section, inferior, I think, to the Benjy motive, though fine in part, describes in the terms of free association with which Mr. Joyce is recreating vocabularies, the final day in this life of Quentin, First, who is contemplating suicide. Quentin is a student at Harvard at the time, the last wealth of the family—some property that has been nominally Benjy's—having been sold to provide him with an education. Quentin is oversensitive, introvert, pathologically devoted to his sister, and his determination to commit suicide is his protest against her disgrace.

In Book III we see the world in terms of the petty, sadistic lunacy of Jason; Jason, the last son of the family, the stay-at-home, the failure, clerking in a country store, for whom no Harvard education was provided. William Faulkner has that general perspective in viewing particular events which lifts the specific incident to the dignity of catholic significance, while all the vividness of an undu-

plicable personal drama is retained. He senses the characteristic
compulsions to action that make a fate. Jason is a devil. Yet, since
the author has compelled you to the vision of the gods, he is a devil
whom you compassionate. Younger than the other brothers, Jason,
in his twenties, is tyrannically compensating for the sufferings of
jealousy by persecution of his young niece, Caddie's daughter,
Quentin, by petty thievery, by deception practiced against his
weak mother, by meanest torment of that marvellously accurately
conceived young negro, Luster, keeper, against all his idle, pleas-
ure-loving inclinations, of the witless Benjy. Jason is going mad.
He knows it—not as an intellectual conclusion, for he holds up
all the emotional barriers against reflection and self-investigation.
Jason knows madness as Benjy knows the world and the smell of
leaves and the leap of the fire in the grate and the sounds of himself, his own howls, when Luster teases him. Madness for Jason is
a blank, immediate state of soul, which he feels encroaching on his
meager, objectively considered universe. He is in an agony of inexplicable anticipation of disaster for which his cruelties afford him
no relief.

The last Book is told in the third person by the author. In its
pages we are to see this small world of failure in its relative aspect.
Especial privilege, we are allowed to meet face to face, Dilsey, the
old colored woman, who provides the beauty of coherence against
the background of struggling choice. Dilsey isn't searching for a
soul. She *is* the soul. She is the conscious human accepting the
limitations of herself, the iron boundaries of circumstance, and
still, to the best of her ability, achieving a holy compromise for
aspiration.

People seem very frequently to ask of a book a "moral." There
is no moral statement in *The Sound and the Fury,* but moral conclusions can be drawn from it as surely as from "life," because, as
fine art, it is life organized to make revelation fuller. Jason is, in
fair measure, the young South, scornful of outworn tradition,
scornful indeed of all tradition, as of the ideal which has betrayed
previous generations to the hope of perfection. He, Jason, would
tell you, as so many others do today, that he sees things "as they
are." There is no "foolishness" about him, no "bunk." A spade is
a spade, as unsuggestive as things must be in an age which prizes
radios and motor cars not as means, but as ends for existence. You
have "got to show him." Where there is no proof in dollars and
cents, or what they can buy, there is nothing. Misconceiving even
biology, Jason would probably regard individualism of a crass order

as according to nature. Jason is a martyr. He is a completely rational being. There is something exquisitely stupid in this degree of commonsense which cannot grasp the fact that ratiocination cannot proceed without presumptions made on the emotional acceptance of a state antedating reason. Jason argues, as it were, from nothing to nothing. In this *reductio ad absurdum* he annihilates himself, even his vanity. And he runs amok, with his conclusion that one gesture is as good as another, that there is only drivelling self-deception to juxtapose to his tin-pot Nietzscheanism—actually the most romantic attitude of all.

But there is Dilsey, without so much as a theory to controvert theory, stoic as some immemorial carving of heroism, going on, doing the best she can, guided only by instinct and affection and the self-respect she will not relinquish—the ideal of herself to which she conforms irrationally, which makes of her life something whole, while her "white folks" accept their fragmentary state, disintegrate. And she recovers for us the spirit of tragedy which the patter of cynicism has often made seem lost.

Preface to *Le Bruit et la fureur*

by *Maurice Coindreau*

"This novel began as a short story," William Faulkner once said to me. "It struck me that it would be interesting to imagine the thoughts of a group of children who were sent away from the house the day of their grandmother's funeral, their curiosity about the activity in the house, their efforts to find out what was going on, and the notions that would come into their minds. Then, to complicate the picture, I had the idea of someone who would be more than just a child, who, in trying to find the answer, would not even have a normal brain to use—that is, an idiot. So Benjy was born. After that, the same thing happened to me that happens to many writers—I fell in love with one of my characters, Caddy. I loved her so much I couldn't decide to give her life just for the duration of the short story. She deserved more than that. So my novel was created, almost in spite of myself. It had no title until one day the familiar words 'the sound and the fury' came to me out of my unconscious. I adopted them immediately, without considering then that the rest of the Shakespearean quotation was a well suited, and maybe better, to my dark story of madness and hatred."

Indeed we find in *Macbeth,* Act V, Scene V, this definition of life: "It is a tale told by an idiot, full of sound and fury, signifying nothing." The first part of William Faulkner's novel is likewise told by an idiot; the entire book vibrates with sound and fury, and will seem devoid of significance to those who hold that a man of letters, each time he takes up his pen, must deliver a message or serve some noble cause. Mr. Faulkner is content to open the gates

"Preface to The Sound and the Fury," *by Maurice Coindreau. Condensed from* The Mississippi Quarterly, *XIX (Summer, 1966), 108-14. Trans. George M. Reeves. The original French preface was printed in* Le Bruit et la fureur *(Paris: Gallimard, 1938). Copyright 1938 by Editions Gallimard; © 1966 by Mississippi State University. Reprinted by permission of the publishers.*

of Hell. He does not force anyone to accompany him, but those who trust him have no cause for regrets. . . .

The structure of *The Sound and the Fury* is essentially musical. Like a composer, Faulkner uses the system of themes. There is not, as in a fugue, a simple theme which develops and undergoes transformations; there are multiple themes which start out, vanish, and reappear to disappear again until the moment they sound forth in all their richness. One thinks of impressionist compositions, mysterious and chaotic on first hearing, but firmly structured beneath their confused appearance. *The Sound and the Fury* is a novel of atmosphere which suggests more than it says, a sort of *Night on Bald Mountain* penetrated by a diabolical wind in which damned souls are whirling, an atrocious poem of hatred with each movement precisely characterized. . . .*

. . . This demoniac symphony . . . lacks only the gaiety of a scherzo, and . . . achieves unity through the help of two elements of equal effectiveness: the cries of Benjy and the noble figure of Dilsey. The cries, which range from wailing to bellowing, play, in Mr. Faulkner's orchestra, the role of percussion instruments with an obsessive rhythm. This is the sonant climate of the novel. The backdrop is the Negroes, resigned witnesses of the extravagances of the whites. Among them Dilsey, black sister of Flaubert's Felicité, is the "simple heart" in all its beauty. Her animal devotion to masters whom she does not judge and her primitive good sense make it possible for her still to hold in her old hand the tiller of this drifting ship which is the Compson house. Negroes abound in contemporary novels of the South, but none attain the moving grandeur of this woman who, not in the least idealized, is, I believe, Mr. Faulkner's most successful creation.

The structure of *The Sound and the Fury* would in itself be enough to discourage the lazy reader. Yet this is not the greatest of the difficulties. William Faulkner knows all the secrets of verbal alchemy. Did not Arnold Bennett say that he wrote like an angel? He knows also the power of the unexpressed. Consequently his style is full of snares. I will mention simply his very curious use of pronouns for which he only rarely gives antecedents (it is always *he* or *she*, without further specification), his use of symbols, and the boldness of his ellipses. . . . I do not hesitate, nevertheless, to affirm

* Coindreau labels the novel's sections or "movements" as follows: Benjy's section—*Moderato;* Quentin's section—*Adagio;* Jason's section—*Allegro;* final section—*Andante religioso, Allegro furioso, Allegro barbaro,* and *Lento.*

that it is not at all necessary to understand every phrase completely in order to savour *The Sound and the Fury.* I would compare the novel to landscapes that improve when seen through an enveloping haze. Its tragic beauty is increased, and its mysteriousness casts a veil over horrors that would lose some of their power if seen in too much direct light. The mind that is contemplative enough to grasp, on a first reading, the meaning of all the enigmas that Faulkner offers us would undoubtedly not experience the impression of conjuration which gives this unique work its greatest charm and its genuine originality.

The Passing of a World

by Irving Howe

The Sound and the Fury records the fall of a house and the death of a society. . . . Perhaps the most remarkable fact about this remarkable novel is that its rich sense of history comes from a story rigidly confined to a single family, a story almost claustrophobic in its concentration on a narrow sequence of events. . . . In *The Sound and the Fury* Faulkner persuades us, as never before, to accept Yoknapatawpha as an emblem of a larger world beyond, and its moral death as an acting-out of the disorder of our time. . . . This book is a lament for the passing of a world, not merely the world of Yoknapatawpha and not merely the South.

The sense of diminution and loss is intensified by Faulkner's setting the action on Good Friday, Saturday, and Easter Sunday, so that the values of the Christian order provide a muted backdrop to the conduct of the Compsons. These Christian references are handled with delicacy and modesty, a triumph of tact Faulkner does not always repeat in his later work. They rarely break past the surface of the story to call attention to themselves and tempt us into the error of allegory; they never deflect us from the behavior and emotions of the represented figures at the center of the book. Toward the end there is a scene in a Negro church, in which all that has happened is brought to a coda by the marvelous sermon of a Negro preacher—"I got de ricklickshun en 'de blood of de Lamb!' "—and the simple kindliness of some Negro figures. Here the foreground action and the Christian references seem to draw closer, not in order to score any religious point or provide critics with occasions for piety, but to allow the language of the Christian

"*The Passing of a World.*" [*Editor's title.*] *From* William Faulkner: A Critical Study, *2nd edition, by Irving Howe. (New York: Random House, Inc., 1962), pp. 46-48, 158-74. Copyright © 1952 by Irving Howe. Condensed and reprinted with the permission of Random House, Inc. In the original, uncondensed essay, Howe, among other things, discusses more fully his reasons for admiring Benjy's section and for criticizing Quentin's section.*

drama, as it has been preserved by the Negroes, to enforce a tacit judgment on the ending of the Compsons. . . .

Since the collapse of the Compson family is to be shown as a completed history, Faulkner can forego the orderly accumulation of suspense that might be had from a conventional narrative. Beginning near the end of his story, he must employ as his first perceiving mind a Compson who has managed to survive until Easter 1928. Mrs. Compson is too silly and Jason too warped to preserve, let alone present, the family history. Quentin is dead, Caddy gone, and Dilsey must be saved for her role as chorus of lament. Only Benjy remains—and this, far from being accidental, is a symbolic token of the book.

Of all the Compsons, Benjy alone is able to retain the past; he alone has not suffered it in conscious experience. . . . He brings no sharply formulated point of view to his memories, in the sense that Quentin and Jason will; his remembering does not organize or condition that which he remembers. To "identify" with Benjy is, therefore, to abandon him as a person and yield oneself to the Compson experience. Yet this abandonment becomes a way of learning to appreciate his role and value. We gain our experience of the Compsons mainly from the materials coursing through his mind, and it is these materials alone that enable us to see that behind his fixed rituals there are genuine meanings, half-forgotten tokens of the past which survive for him as realities of the present. . . . The pattern of order to which he is so attached may signify nothing in itself, nor need the pain consequent on its disruption signify anything—unless there are those present who understand and can remember what Benjy clings to. Without knowing observers, Benjy is simply the past forsaken. None of the Compsons has remained to care and only Jason so much as remembers; soon it is we, the alien readers, who together with Dilsey must take the burden on ourselves. Only then can we understand Benjy. . . .

Though the last section contains a few incidents not anticipated in the earlier ones, these are merely bitter footnotes to a text of disaster; almost everything else is foreshadowed by Benjy. *The Sound and the Fury* does not launch an action through a smooth passage of time; it reconstructs a history through a suspension—or several suspensions—of time. In the water-splashing incident to which Benjy persistently returns, the behavior of the Compson children is an innocent anticipation of their destinies; each shows himself as he will later become. The Benjy section thus forms not merely one part or one movement among four, but the hard nucleus of the novel. Later sections will add to the pathos of Quentin's reflections and the treachery of Jason's conduct, but merely as variations or extensions of what has already been present from the beginning. . . .

Benjy is a risk. His section could easily become sentimental or incoherent or a pointless flaunting of ingenuity; it is saved from such failings by the fact that he never ceases to be an idiot, never becomes aware of his enormous pathos, never falls into mere shrewdness or saintliness. . . . Faulkner is never in greater command of his material than in the Benjy section, nor more devoted to the classical principles of rigor, impersonality, and austerity than in this most experimental of his writings. . . .

That Benjy's flow of memory must be accepted as a convention rather than as "real" makes Faulkner's success all the more remarkable. The reflections of Quentin Compson can be attributed to an actual man, and Jason's too; but not those of Benjy. Little is known of idiots, and the little that is known suggests that their "thoughts" are a good deal more fragmented and incoherent than Benjy's. For all its complexity, the Benjy section is an extreme simplification, probably difficult to justify by any standard of strict verisimilitude. It hardly matters. Faulkner is concerned not with the mental life of an actual idiot, but with rendering a plausible effect: a flow of disturbed memory which, in the absence of contrary knowledge, can be associated with an idiot.

To picture this disturbed flow of memory one must assume that it makes sense, that an order inheres in it or can profitably be drawn from it. The impression Faulkner seeks to establish, at least the first one, is that Benjy's memories are formless; yet only through precise form can this impression take root and thrive in the reader's mind. Satisfying the needs of both character and author, a simulation of disorder comes to convey an order of significance.

Toward this end Faulkner drafts all his ingenuity, and refrains, moreover, from the rhetorical bombardments that mar a number of his other books. Self-effacing and rigidly disciplined, he directs his language to the uses of his subject, and the result is that his writing is more delicate and controlled than anywhere else in his work. He stakes everything on elemental presentation. He avoids complex sentence structures explicitly involving logic, sequence, and qualification. In place of an elaborate syntax, there is a march of short declarative sentences and balanced compounds following the journey of Benjy's senses. Monotony is the obvious risk of this grammatical stripping, but it is escaped in several ways: frequent time shifts in Benjy's memories, a richness of concrete pictorial imagery, and an abundance of sharply inflected voices. The internal regularity of individual sentences is thus played off against the subtle pacing and tonal variety of the sequence as a whole—the sentences invoking Benjy and the sequence that which exists beyond Benjy. Though the rhythm and shape of the sentences vary but little, there is a wide range of speed. Beginning with relatively large units, Benjy's memories break into increasingly small fragments until, at the climax, brief sentences of recalled incident whirl feverishly about one another, mixing events from 1898, 1910, and 1928. And then the agitated spinning of Benjy's mind comes to an abrupt stop, resting in memories of childhood.

No elaborate similes or metaphors, no hyperbole or euphuism; the few symbols are worked with niggardly concentration, and, thereby, with all the greater effectiveness. Pared and precise, eluding abstraction and reverie, the writing absorbs its color from the life it appropriates, the pictures of behavior and accents of speech. It favors concreteness and spareness, particularly nouns naming common objects, and adjectives specifying blunt sensations.

Through such nouns and adjectives Faulkner manages his transitions in time. Places, names, smells, feelings—these are the chance stimuli that switch Benjy from one track of memory to another. As they impress themselves on him, jolting his mind backward or forward in time, they seem mere accidental distractions, and it is important for the credibility of the section that they continue to seem so; but they are also carefully spaced and arranged so as to intensify Faulkner's meanings by effects of association, incongruity and, above all, juxtaposition.

Juxtaposition is here both method and advantage. Through it we gain sudden insights and shocks which, in small symbolic presentiments or recapitulations, crystallize the meanings of the sequence. . . . By making the past seem simultaneous with the present, Faulkner gains remarkable moments of pathos, moments sounding the irrevocable sadness that comes from a recognition of decline and failure. And remarkable, one must add, for the way small incidents and contrasts, little more than the slurred minutiae of life, suggest the largest issues in human conduct. . . . In each of these juxtapositions, the whole Compson story is enacted: in Mrs. Compson's whining over her "baby," in the treatment of Benjy by his sister and niece, in the varying significance the gate has for Benjy. Such contrasts reveal the family's history in all its vulnerability, and the result is not an account but a picture of experience, a series of stripped exposures. When Benjy's mind comes to rest, the final effect of these juxtapositions is overwhelming. To specify that effect accurately requires a somewhat startling comparison. In Jane Austen's *Persuasion* the writing forms a highly polished and frequently trivial surface of small talk, and only toward the end does one fully realize that beneath this surface has occurred a romance of exquisite refinement. In the Benjy section, the writing forms a surface that is rough, broken, and forbidding, and only toward the end does one fully realize that beneath it Faulkner has retrieved a social history of exquisite pathos. At opposite poles of technique, the two pieces have in common an essential trait of art: they reveal more than they say. . . .

. . . The Benjy section, by picturing a disintegration specific to one family yet common to our age, gains its strength from a largeness of reference. The Quentin section abruptly reduces the scope of the novel to a problem that is "special" in a clinical sense and not necessarily an equivalent or derivative of the Compson history. Where Benjy recalls a world, Quentin nurses an obsession. . . . I doubt that even the strictest Christian moralist could suppose Quentin's chastity neurosis a satisfactory embodiment of the tragic themes announced and developed in the Benjy section. I would also doubt that Quentin can sustain the weight some critics have thrust upon him: the weight of a search for standards of conduct and value in a world that has not only lost them but no longer cares about the loss. In his own pitiable way Quentin is engaged in such a quest; some hunger for an informing sense of principle surely lies behind his lostness; but to say this, unfortunately, is not to reconcile us to his part in the novel, for too often his quest shrinks disastrously to mere nostalgia, forcing us to notice the discrepancy between what he is and what he is supposed to signify. . . . The one character who struggles toward an inclusive view of his family history, Quentin must in some way be seen as a morally aware person, not merely as a psychological case. . . . He tries hard and the effort is frequently touching, but his obsession finally bars him from understanding fully the nature and dimension of the Compson tragedy. Quentin is too weak, too passive, too bewildered for the role of sensitive hero. Benjy, though an idiot, reveals the family situation more faithfully than Quentin, for the events Benjy remembers tell us more than the efforts of Quentin to comprehend them. Or to put it another way, Quentin does not add enough to what the Benjy section has already provided.

This comparison may be reinforced by a glance at the symbolic patterns of the two sections. Because the few symbols in the Benjy section are imbedded within or arise from the action itself, they seem organic and spontaneous, while the far more numerous symbols of the Quentin section are often arbitrary, scattered in effect and literary in source. It is a difference between craftsmanship and literary self-consciousness, between symbols working on the reader's sensibility and symbols aggressively thrust before his eyes. . . .*

More could be said about Faulkner's use of symbols; it may be better to say that they are often a mare's nest for critics. The contemporary eagerness to interpret works of literature as symbolic patterns is often due to a fear or distaste of direct experience—sometimes, of direct literary experience. . . . When hardened into critical dogma, this mode of interpretation supports the assumption that truth or reality is always "behind" what we see and sense—that an essence lurks in the phenomenon, a ghost in the machine, a spirit in the tree. . . . Yet what would the symbols of *The Sound and the Fury* matter? How could they stir our emotions? Were they not subordinate to Faulkner's power in rendering pictures and recording voices? Symbolic patterns certainly appear in the novel, and important ones; but their importance depends on the primary presence of represented objects and people. As an instance of this pictorial mastery, here is Dilsey, an old woman on a Sunday morning:

> She wore a stiff black straw hat perched upon her turban, and a maroon velvet cape with a border of mangy and anonymous fur above a dress of purple silk, and she stood in the door for awhile with her myriad and sunken face lifted to the weather, and one gaunt hand flac-soled as the belly of a fish, then she moved the cape aside and examined the bosom of her gown.

. . . To speak of greatness with regard to one's contemporaries is dangerous. But if there are any American novels of the present century which may be called great, which bear serious comparison with the achievements of twentieth-century European literature, then surely *The Sound and the Fury* is among them. It is one of the three or four American works of prose fiction written since the turn of the century in which the impact of tragedy is felt and sustained. Seized by his materials, Faulkner keeps, for once, within

---

* In extending this argument, Howe criticizes the references to Hamlet and the clock symbolism in Quentin's section; but he praises Faulkner's symbolic use of honeysuckle in this section, of money in Jason's section, and of golf balls and death motifs in Benjy's section.

his esthetic means. *The Sound and the Fury* is the one novel in which his vision and technique are almost in complete harmony, and the vision itself whole and major. Whether taken as a study of the potential for human self-destruction, or as a rendering of the social disorder particular to our time, the novel projects a radical image of man against the wall.

Worlds in Counterpoint

by Olga W. Vickery

The Sound and the Fury was the first of Faulkner's novels to
make the question of form and technique an unavoidable critical
issue. In any discussion of its structure the controlling assumption
should be that there are plausible reasons for the particular arrangement of the four sections and for the use of the stream of consciousness technique in the first three and not in the fourth. Jean-Paul
Sartre's comment that the moment the reader attempts to isolate
the plot content "he notices that he is telling another story" indicates the need for such an assumption, not only for any light that
may be thrown on *The Sound and the Fury* but for any insight that
may emerge concerning Faulkner's method and achievement.

The structure of the novel is clearly reflected in the organization of the events of the evening on which Damuddy dies. These
events reveal the typical gestures and reactions of the four children
to each other and to the mysterious advent of death. They chart
the range and kind of each of their responses to a new experience.
In this way the evening partakes of the dual nature of the novel:
primarily it is an objective, dramatic scene revealing the relations
and tensions which exist among the children, but at the same time
it is a study in perspective. Between the fact of Damuddy's death
and the reader stands not only the primitive mind of the narrator,

"Worlds in Counterpoint," by Olga W. Vickery. From The Novels of William
Faulkner: A Critical Introduction (*Baton Rouge: Louisiana State University
Press, 1959; rev. edition 1964*), Chap. 3. Originally printed as "The Sound and
the Fury: A Study in Perspective," Publications of the Modern Language Association, LXIX (*December, 1954*), 1017-37. Condensed and reprinted with permission from PMLA and the Louisiana State University Press. Copyright ©
1954 by PMLA; copyright © 1959 and 1964 by the Louisiana State University
Press. In the original, uncondensed essay, Mrs. Vickery gives a more detailed
analysis of Quentin's attempt "to coerce experience into conformity with his
system" and offers many more examples of Jason's "calculating" or "legalistic"
approach to experience.

Benjy, but the diverse attitudes of the other children and the deliberate uncommunicativeness of the adults.

Within the novel as a whole it is Caddy's surrender to Dalton Ames which serves both as the source of dramatic tension and as the focal point for the various perspectives. This is evident in the fact that the sequence of events is not caused by her act—which could be responded to in very different ways—but by the significance which each of her brothers actually attributes to it. As a result, the four sections appear quite unrelated even though they repeat certain incidents and are concerned with the same problem, namely Caddy and her loss of virginity. Although there is a progressive revelation or rather clarification of the plot, each of the sections is itself static. The consciousness of each character becomes the actual agent illuminating and being illuminated by the central situation. Everything is immobilized in this pattern; there is no development of either character or plot in the traditional manner. This impression is reinforced not only by the shortness of time directly involved in each section but by the absence of any shifts in style of the kind that, for example, accompany the growing maturity of Cash Bundren in *As I Lay Dying*.

By fixing the structure while leaving the central situation ambiguous, Faulkner forces the reader to reconstruct the story and to apprehend its significance for himself. Consequently, the reader recovers the story at the same time as he grasps the relation of Benjy, Quentin, and Jason to it. This, in turn, is dependent on his comprehension of the relation between the present and the past events with which each of the first three sections deals. As he proceeds from one section to the next, there is a gradual clarification of events, a rounding out of the fragments of scenes and conversations which Benjy reports. Thus, with respect to the plot the four sections are inextricably connected, but with respect to the central situation they are quite distinct and self-sufficient. As related to the central focus, each of the first three sections presents a version of the same facts which is at once the truth and a complete distortion of the truth. It would appear, then, that the theme of *The Sound and the Fury*, as revealed by the structure, is the relation between the act and man's apprehension of the act, between the event and the interpretation. The relation is by no means a rigid or inelastic thing but is a matter of shifting perspective, for, in a sense, each man creates his own truth. This does not mean that truth does not exist or that it is fragmentary or that it is unknowable; it only insists that truth is a matter of the heart's response as well as the mind's logic.

In keeping with this theme each of the first three sections presents a well demarcated and quite isolated world built around one of these splinters of truth. The fact that Benjy is dumb is symbolic of the closed nature of these worlds; communication is impossible when Caddy who is central to all three means something different to each. For Benjy she is the smell of trees; for Quentin, honor; and for Jason, money or at least the means of obtaining it. Yet these intense private dramas are taking place in a public world primarily concerned with observable behavior. Accordingly, in the fourth section we are shown what an interested but unimplicated observer would see of the Compsons. For the first time we realize that Benjy has blue eyes, that Mrs. Compson habitually wears black dressing gowns, and that Jason looks somewhat like a caricature of a bartender. Moreover, since we are prevented from sharing in the consciousness and memories of the characters, Caddy is no longer an immediate center. Nevertheless, through the conflict between Jason and Miss Quentin the final repercussions of her affair penetrate into the life of Jefferson and even Mottson. And out of the Compson house, itself a symbol of isolation, one person, Dilsey, emerges to grasp the truth which must be felt as well as stated.

Out of the relation that Benjy, Quentin, and Jason bear to Caddy yet another pattern emerges: a gradual progression from the completely closed and private world of the first section to the completely public world of the fourth. . . . Moreover, each of these shifts from the private to the public world is accompanied by a corresponding shift in the form of apprehension. With Benjy we are restricted entirely to sensation which cannot be communicated; quite appropriately therefore Benjy is unable to speak. . . . Quentin's world is almost as isolated and inflexible as Benjy's, but its order is based on abstractions rather than sensations. While Benjy can comprehend only the physical aspects of his experience, Quentin sees the physical only as a manifestation of ideas. Thus, his section is filled with echoes, both literary and Biblical, phrases, names quoted out of context but falling neatly into the pattern of his thought. These echoes assume the quality of a ritual by which he attempts to conjure experience into conformity with his wishes. . . . The third section shows a greater degree of clarity though not of objectivity. The reason for this is that Jason operates in terms of a logic which forms the basis of social communication. . . . It is part of the general satiric intent of this section that Jason's obvious distortion of Caddy should be associated with logic and reason. . . . The objective nature of the fourth section precludes the use of any single level of apprehension, and accordingly it provokes the most complex response. Dilsey, almost as inarticulate as Benjy, becomes through her actions alone the embodiment of the truth of the heart which is synonymous with morality. . . . To use Dilsey as a point of view character would be to destroy her efficacy as the ethical norm, for that would give us but one more splinter of the truth confined and conditioned by the mind which grasped it. . . .

Our first impression of the Benjy section is that it presents a state of utter chaos for which the only possible justification is the fact that Benjy is an idiot and therefore has the right to be confused. But out of this disorder two patterns emerge: the one, completely independent of public perspective, constitutes Benjy's world, the other serves as the author's guide for enabling the reader to grasp the fragments as a comprehensible order. With respect to the latter, critics have pointed out both Faulkner's use of italics to indicate shifts in time and the fact that the reasons for such shifts occurring are easily recognizable. An object, a sound, an incident may propel the mind toward some point in the past where a similar experience took place.

Equally important is the fact that there are actually very few scenes involved despite the length of time covered. The events of 7 April 1928 are easily identified because of the prominence given to Luster in them. His dogged and somewhat querulous search for the lost quarter and his single-minded preoccupation with the show run like an identifying motif in a difficult composition. Otherwise, there are but three extended episodes: one taking place some time in 1898, the day Damuddy died; the second occurring on the evening Benjy received his new name; and the last consisting of the scene of Caddy's wedding. Each of these episodes has its own principle of organization. Benjy's other recollections create the impression of a mind confused and undiscriminating, but they are for the most part short, self-sufficient vignettes. At times these unit-episodes interlock as when Benjy's intrusion into Miss Quentin's privacy on the swing recalls a similar scene involving Caddy. In this case the recollected event is completed before we are returned to the present scene of Miss Quentin's anger and her friend's perverse humor.

The organization of the fragments in the first main episode is more complex but none the less comprehensible. Large sections of the time between 1898 and 1928 are marked off by the succession of Benjy's nurses and thus some sort of relative chronology can be established as we shift from Versh to T.P. to Luster. But more important is the fact that the pieces forming the scene beginning at the Branch and ending with the children's reactions to Damuddy's death are only interrupted by other pieces and not themselves dislocated in time. If it were possible to blot out these intrusive scenes, we would have the events of that day in a chronological order. Yet since there can be a double shift in one of the interrupting passages, both of which are indicated by italics, the continuity of the single day has to be established by other means.

Accordingly, we have a succession of verbal clues which show that the interruption is over. For example, a train of recollection begins when Luster allows Benjy to play in the water and Benjy remembers the earlier scene when all the Compson children were playing at the Branch under the somewhat uncertain supervision of Versh: *"and Roskus came and said to come to supper and Caddy said, It's not supper time yet."* (37) Just when he remembers Caddy promising not to run away, Luster breaks in with his impatient scolding, and this is immediately followed by the verbal echo: "Roskus came and said to come to supper and Caddy said it wasn't supper time yet." (39) A number of the scenes from the day of Damuddy's death are identified by references to the buzzards who have "undressed" Nancy or to the bottle of lightning bugs which Benjy carries. But again paired sentences are used to indicate resumption of the episode. "Versh took me up and we went on around the kitchen" (56) is picked up by "We stopped under the tree by the parlor window. Versh set me down in the wet grass." (57) This careful interweaving of the fragments, evident throughout the whole episode, is supported and its efficacy increased by the fact that most of the interrupting passages are too short to interfere with our recognition of the linking phrase.

The scattered pieces of the wedding scene are identified mainly by T.P.'s inebriated antics and his prowess with "sassprilluh" but also, of course, by Caddy's "long veil like shining wind." These provide sufficient clues since we are concerned with a single scene rather than a succession of events. The evening on which Maury is renamed Benjy gains its unity through the use of repeated sensations rather than echo words. Each fragment of the evening is marked by some reference to the sound of rain or the presence of the fire. Eventually the mirror, which by itself is not a sufficient clue since it is also associated with Caddy's wedding, becomes a secondary means of identification as Benjy watches all the actions of the Compsons reflected in its surface. A somewhat similar use of sensations is found in the episode which begins with Benjy's waiting for Caddy and ends with their visit to Mrs. Patterson. Here the sign is a reference either to the coldness of the weather or to Benjy's propensity for getting his hands frozen.

With consummate skill the repetitions and identifying sensations which are used to guide the reader are also used as the basis of Benjy's own ordering of experience. Benjy's mind works not by association which is dependent, to some extent, on an ability to discriminate as well as compare but by mechanical identification. Thus, being caught on the fence while walking with Luster does not recall an associated feeling or fact but the exact replica of the incident. More important is the fact that the three deaths in the family, which Benjy senses are repetitions of each other, provoke an identical response. What he reacts to is the fact of death or the fact of being caught on the fence. To differentiate in terms of time and circumstance is a logical matter and therefore beyond Benjy's range of apprehension.

This is further illustrated by his inflexible identification of one word with one object. Very seldom, for example, is the name of a speaker replaced by a pronoun in his section. Each person is freed from the multiplicity of descriptive relations which make him at once man and brother, father, Negro or white. For Benjy, he is forever fixed as simply Jason, Quentin, or Luster. In the one scene where Benjy is brought into contact with Luster's friends, parts of the dialogue are consistently attributed to Luster, but the answers appear to come out of the air. Benjy does not know the names of these strangers and to give them an identity in terms of description is beyond his power. His literalism finds its sharpest illustration in the scene where the cries of the golfers are heard. "Caddy" can mean only one thing and elicit only one response.

Benjy both orders and evaluates his experience with this same rigidity. The objects he has learned to recognize constitute an inflexible pattern which he defends against novelty or change with every bellow in his overgrown body. At what time or under what circumstances the small mound of earth which Dilsey calls his graveyard was formed and marked with two empty bottles of blue glass holding withered stalks of jimson weed is unimportant. But that this arrangement, once established, should remain unchanged in the slightest detail is of the utmost importance. When Luster removes one of the bottles, Benjy is momentarily shocked into a

silence which is immediately succeeded by a roar of protest. It is
not that the bottle has any intrinsic value for Benjy, but merely
that it forms part of the pattern which must not be disturbed. The
fixed route to the graveyard is also sacred; Benjy is overwhelmed
with horror and agony when Luster takes the wrong turn only to
subside the minute the mistake is corrected.

Within this rigid world Caddy is at once the focus of order and
the instrument of its destruction. The pasture, the fire, and sleep,
the three things Benjy loves most, are associated with her . . .
Caddy both realizes and respects his fear of change. . . . Yet what
Benjy most expects of Caddy is the one thing she cannot give him,
for his expectation is based on his complete indifference to or
rather ignorance of time. As long as Caddy is in time, she cannot
free herself from change. His dependence on her physical presence,
her scent of trees, is subject to constant threats which he fends off
to the best of his ability. The intensity of his reaction is caused by
the fact that any alteration in Caddy makes her not-Caddy. Thus,
Caddy, as in the Quentin section, is at once identified with the rigid
order of Benjy's private world and with the disorder of actual
experience. Depending on which of the two is dominant at the
moment, Benjy moans or smiles serenely. . . .

. . . Quentin too has constructed for himself a private world
to which Caddy is essential, a world which is threatened and finally
destroyed by her involvement in circumstance. . . . Whereas Benjy
is saved by being outside time, Quentin is destroyed by his excessive
awareness of it. For the former, both the pattern and its disordering
are eternally present as his alternation between moaning and smil-
ing demonstrates; for the latter, the pattern has become a part of
the past and contentment has been replaced by despair. Quentin can
neither accept nor reconcile himself to that change or to the possibility that a further change may make even his despair a thing of
the past, and so he chooses death as a means of escaping the situation.

The structure of the section with its two sets of events, one past
and the other present, reflects Quentin's problem. Throughout the
day he can proceed quite mechanically with such chores as getting
dressed, packing, writing letters, and generally tidying up the
loose ends of his life at Harvard. To a large extent he can even
make the appropriate gestures and speak the proper words expected
of him by others. Meanwhile, his mind is occupied with echoes of
the past which make themselves felt with increasing intensity until
they threaten to prevent even a mechanical attention to the details

of living through that final day. Quentin cannot escape either his memories of the past or his involvement in the present. . . .

The order which Quentin had once built around Caddy is as rigid and inflexible as Benjy's and it shares Benjy's fear of change and his expectation that all experience should conform to his pattern. The cause of his ineffectuality and his ultimate destruction is the fact that his system antecedes his experience and eventually is held in defiance of experience. His is an ethical order based on words, on "fine, dead sound," the meaning of which he has yet to learn. He has, in short, separated ethics from the total context of humanity. Insofar as virginity is a concept, associated with virtue and honor, it becomes the center of Quentin's world, and since it is also physically present in Caddy, it forms a precarious link between his world and that of experience. Mr. Compson remarks that virginity is merely a transient physical state which has been given its ethical significance by men. What they have chosen to make it mean is something which is a defiance of nature, an artificial isolation of the woman. Caddy, who seems almost a symbol of the blind forces of nature, is an unstable guardian for that "concept of Compson honor precariously and . . . only temporarily supported by the minute fragile membrane of her maidenhead." Quentin can only try to buttress it with more words, with "some presbyterian concept of . . . eternal punishment." Since his emotional responses center on these concepts, Quentin is quite incapable of love for any human being, even Caddy. Despite his feverish preoccupation with ethics, he is unable to perform any ethical actions himself; even his death is not so much a protest as it is simply a withdrawal. Thus, it is not the time that is out of joint but Quentin's relation to time. . . .

The symbols and recurrent phrases that run through Quentin's section both intensify the emotional impact and reinforce the meaning. Such names as Jesus, St. Francis, Moses, Washington, and Byron not only add a richness of historical and literary allusion but convey the nature of Quentin's world. Into that world Benjy is admitted as "Benjamin the child of mine old age held hostage into Egypt" and Caddy as Eve or Little Sister Death. Mr. Compson forces an entry not as father or friend but as a voice which can juggle words and ideas while insisting on their emptiness. As for Quentin, he sees himself as the hero of the family drama, the "bitter prophet and inflexible corruptless judge." (10) Part of his outrage and frustration in connection with Caddy is that neither her husband nor her lover seems worthy, in his eyes, of assuming a role in his world: Herbert is obviously despicable and Ames refuses to act in terms of Quentin's preconceptions.

The heavy, choking fragrance of honeysuckle dramatizes the conflict between his order and the blind forces of nature which constantly threaten to destroy it. Honeysuckle is the rife animality of sex, the incomprehensible and hateful world for which Caddy has abandoned his paradise, and hence it is also the symbol of his defeat. Yet honeysuckle is only a sensation, just as Caddy's affair with Ames is simply a natural event. It is Quentin who makes of the one a symbol of "night and unrest" and of the other the unforgivable sin. . . .

The constant references to the shadows and the mirror emphasize the barrier between Quentin and reality. It is not only Benjy but also Quentin who sees Caddy's wedding reflected in the mirror. Caddy, however, cannot be confined to its surface; she runs out of the mirror and out of his and Benjy's world. Similarly, Quentin sees her and Ames not as people but as silhouettes distorted against the sky. He is lost amid these shadows, feeling that they falsify the objects they pretend to reflect, yet unable to reach out beyond them. It is significant that he sees only those aspects of Caddy as shadows which he cannot incorporate into his world: it is her love affair and her marriage which he finds perverse, mocking, denying the significance they should have affirmed. The same feeling of mockery is present in his insistence that he has tricked his shadow. A man who is dead needs no shadow, but still his accompanies him throughout the day as if it were mirroring reality when in truth it is but aping another illusion.

The number of times that the shadow images are fused with images of water indicates that death by water is Quentin's way of reconciling his two worlds, of merging shadow and reality and tempering their conflict. Whatever suggestion of purification may be present, water is primarily a symbol of oblivion for Quentin. Both Quentin and Caddy run to the Branch to surrender themselves to its hypnotic rhythm which, like sleep, soothes the mind into unconsciousness, blurring thought and emotion, eliminating the necessity for acting. It is in the hope of making this peace eternal that Quentin surrenders his body to the water where the hard knots of circumstance will be untangled and the roof of wind will stand forever between him and the loud world.

With Jason's section we enter a world far different from Benjy's or Quentin's yet related to theirs through Caddy. It represents a third possible way of reacting to experience, as distorted yet as "true" as the former two. Since Jason reacts logically rather than emotionally, his section offers no barriers to comprehension. His particular method of ordering and explaining his action in terms of cause and effect, profit and loss, is all too familiar. Yet logic, presumably the basis of human communication and hence of society, isolates Jason as effectively as the moral abstractions of Quentin or the complete dependence on sensations of Benjy. In the midst of Jefferson or even his family, he is by necessity as well as by choice alone. . . .

One of Jason's dominant characteristics, and the main source of humor, is his pride that he has no illusions about his family or himself. . . . The conviction that he alone has a firm grasp on reality results in a literalism untouched by any hint of qualification in Jason's thinking. . . . It is his very insistence on facing facts that causes his distorted view of Caddy, his family, and the whole human race. He cannot imagine that there might be other facts, other aspects of the situation, than the ones that directly affect him; as a result, he sees certain things so clearly that all others escape him. . . . His is a world reduced to calculation in which no subjective claims are tolerated and no margin for error allowed. This calculating approach to experience pervades his every act, no matter how trivial. . . . All [his] arrangements constitute Jason's way of protecting himself from any intrusion of the irrational. It is his method of assuming control over experience by preventing himself from becoming involved in circumstances he has not foreseen. . . . During his frantic pursuit of Miss Quentin the nature of the conflict in which Jason is involved becomes explicit. He realizes that his enemy is not his niece or even the man with the red tie; rather it is "the sequence of natural events and their causes which shadows every mans brow." . . .

In the last section we finally emerge from the closed world of the Compson Mile into the public world as represented by Jefferson. No longer colored by the subjectivity of a single point of view, the outward manifestations of appearance and behavior assume a new importance. We are still permitted occasional glimpses of Jason's mind but only as he reacts to experience and not as he attempts to control it. The primary result is that the whole history of the Compsons is given a wider reference. Absence and time have erased Caddy and Quentin from the scene, even if the promiscuity of the one and the suicide of the other originally had an impact beyond the family. And Caddy, at any rate, never existed in the novel except in the minds and memories of those whom she had

affected. In this larger context the sound and the fury of the family
signifies very little if anything. . . .

In this section Dilsey emerges not only as a Negro servant in the
Compson household but as a human being. With nothing to judge
but her actions, with no prolonged ethical or religious polemics,
her very presence enables the reader to achieve a final perspective
on the lives of the Compsons. Mrs. Compson's nagging self-pity,
Jason's carping exactions, Miss Quentin's thoughtlessness gain a
dramatic actuality lacking while they were being filtered through
an individual consciousness. Various contrasts between Dilsey and
the others are delineated with striking clarity. The contrast becomes actual conflict where Dilsey and Jason are concerned. It is
not only that Dilsey "survives," because, for that matter, so does
Jason, but that her endurance has strength to suffer without rancor
as well as to resist, to accept as well as to protest. She is the only
one who challenges his word in the household, who defends the
absent Caddy, Miss Quentin, Benjy, and even Luster from his
anger. But more important, she challenges the validity and efficacy
of his world by a passive and irrational resistance to which he has
no counter. That someone should work without pay is so foreign
to his system that he is helpless in the face of it.

There is no doubt but that Dilsey is meant to represent the
ethical norm, the realizing and acting out of one's humanity; it is
from this that the Compsons have deviated, each into his separate
world. The mother and her two elder sons have abandoned their
humanity for the sake of pride or vanity or self-pity. Both Benjy
and Caddy are tests of the family's humanity, he simply because
he is not fully human and she because her conduct creates a socio-
moral hiatus between the family and Jefferson. Benjy's behavior
is a constant trial to the family and to this extent counterpoints
Caddy's lone disgracing act. Both challenge the family's capacity
for understanding and forgiveness and the family fails both. Quite
appropriately, the Compson Mile exists in an atmosphere not only
of disintegration but of constriction. The property shrinks as the
town begins "to encroach and then nibble at and into it." (7) The
only room which seems to be lived in is Dilsey's kitchen; the others
are so many private mausoleums. While each of the Compsons to
some extent attempts to coerce experience and to deny his involvement in the sequence of natural events and their causes, Dilsey
accepts whatever time brings. She alone never suffers that moment
of rejection which is equated with death.

By working with circumstance instead of against it she creates order out of disorder; by accommodating herself to change she manages to keep the Compson household in some semblance of decency. While occupied with getting breakfast, she is yet able to start the fire in Luster's inexplicable absence, provide a hot water bottle for Mrs. Compson, see to Benjy's needs, and soothe various ruffled tempers. All this despite the constant interruptions of Luster's perverseness, Benjy's moaning, Mrs. Compson's complaints, and even Jason's maniacal fury. The same calmness is evident with regard to Caddy's affair, Quentin's suicide, and the arrival of Caddy's baby. As she herself states, she has brought up Caddy and can do the same for Miss Quentin. And if it so happens that their conduct mocks all her care and love, then it is time to find another order in the subsequent confusion. Dilsey's attitude, as she lives it, is formed by her instinctive feeling that whatever happens must be met with courage and dignity in which there is no room for passivity or pessimism.

Her ability to stand steadfast without faltering in the face of circumstance finds further expression in her patient preoccupation with the present, which is the only possible way of living with time. This does not imply that Dilsey is cut off from the past but only that she deals with it as it is caught up in the present without attempting to perpetuate a part of it as Quentin does, or to circumvent it as Jason tries to do. In a sense, she is a living record of all that has happened to the Compsons made significant by her own strength and courage. It is a record of pain and suffering and change but also of endurance and permanence in change.

In describing Dilsey as an ethical norm it should be stressed that she propounds no system, no code of behavior or belief, and this despite the emphasis on the Easter service which she attends. Neither in her attitude nor in the service itself is there any reference to sin and punishment but only to suffering and its surcease. At no time does Dilsey judge any of the Compsons, not even Jason, though she does object at one point to those who frown on Benjy's presence in a Negro church. But her presence enables the reader to judge not systems but actions and hence to grasp the truth instinctively: "They [Negroes] come into white people's lives like that in sudden sharp black trickles that isolate white facts for an instant in unarguable truth like under a microscope." (189) And though she does not judge, Dilsey is never deceived; her comprehension of the relations between Caddy and the rest of the family is unerring.

Dilsey's participation in the Easter service is the one meaningful ritual in the book. As she proceeds sedately from house to church, acknowledging greetings with proper reserve and dignity, she is still conscious of being, in some sense, a member of the Compson household with a certain prestige and obligations. With each member of the congregation similarly conscious of his own distinctive position in society, the Reverend Shegog begins using the magic of his voice. When he concludes, communication has been replaced by communion in which each member loses his identity but finds his humanity and the knowledge that all men are equal and brothers in their suffering.

Out of Dilsey's actions and her participation in the Easter service arise once more the simple verities of human life, which Faulkner's Stockholm address describes as "the old universal truths lacking which any story is ephemeral and doomed—love and honor and pity and pride and compassion and sacrifice." It is these truths which throw the final illumination not only on Caddy and the whole sequence of events that started with her affair but also on what each of the Compsons believed her to be. The splinters of truth presented in the first three sections reverberate with the sound and the fury signifying nothing. But out of those same events, the same disorder and confusion, come Dilsey's triumph and her peace, lending significance not only to her own life but to the book as a whole.

Concepts of Time in *The Sound and the Fury*

by Perrin Lowrey

Throughout *The Sound and the Fury* clocks and watches and references to time provide a ticking refrain to the central action. . . . Each of [the major characters] holds an idea of time which is appropriate to the theme Faulkner wishes to express and which serves the total structure he has created as well. . . . In the final structure the characters' time concepts are correlated artistically with the various time devices which serve the telling of the story. . . .

It is apparent that there are two actions, which have different time spans. One action takes place on April 6, 7, and 8 of the year 1928—it is an action which revolves around Jason and Miss Quentin. He antagonizes her; she steals his hoarded money and runs away; Jason chases her. This action is minor, though it is climactic and stems directly from the major action. But more important, the three-day action serves as a framework about which Faulkner can hang a larger—and much more complex—action; an action which embraces thirty years' time. The large action begins in 1898, when the Compson children were small, and ends on April 8, 1928. . . .

Essentially . . . the distinction to be made is between the action and the way in which the action is represented. If we consider as the major action all the important events that have happened in the Compson household over a generation, then the three-day action can be considered not only as climax but also as device, a means, one of the special techniques he uses to get his story told.

"Concepts of Time in The Sound and the Fury," *by Perrin Lowrey. From* English Institute Essays, 1952, *ed. Alan S. Downer (New York: Columbia University Press, 1954), pp. 57-82. Copyright © 1954, by the Columbia University Press. Condensed and reprinted with permission from the publisher. In the original, uncondensed essay, Lowrey, among other things, discusses more fully the arrangement of the four sections, the order and function of the dislocated time sequences, and the "cyclical" progression that begins and ends the novel with Benjy.*

Such a distinction leads us to another interesting observation about the chronology of the novel. Although Ben's mind ranges over the whole period of the major action, 1898 to 1928, the emphasis of his thought is on the period 1899 to 1910. Ben recalls only a few scenes which occur after 1910; he thinks only once or twice of things that happened in 1912, 1913, and 1915. He thinks most about his early childhood, the period from 1899 to 1905. In one sense, then, the novel, though apparently chaotic, is actually roughly chronological. Ben deals with the time around 1900 primarily, Quentin is obsessed with the events leading up to 1910, Jason's thoughts are focussed for the most part on the events between 1910 and 1928 (with an emphasis on the present), and the final section deals with 1928 exclusively. . . .

. . . If we put aside the intricate structure, what we see is the decline of a particular sort of Southern family. The Compsons, once a family proud and great, come to a terrible end. . . . The "curse" on the House of Compson has seemed obscure to most critics. The characters themselves explain it only superficially— Quentin says it is the "bad blood of the Bascombs"; Caddy says simply that they are cursed, and does not even pretend to know why; Old Man Compson thinks all men are cursed.

But when we begin to examine the concepts of time which Ben, Jason, and Quentin hold, some of the difficulty with motivation disappears. Each of the Compson sons has a concept of time which makes it difficult for him to live in his world. And these concepts of time are essentially signs to the reader, symptoms of something within the Compsons which brings each of them to final ruin. Only one person in the novel—Dilsey—escapes the wreckage of the crumbling house, and it is Dilsey . . . who holds a proper notion of time, who understands that time is a continuum. . . .

To speak of Ben's concept of time is in reality a contradiction, for Ben cannot conceive of time. For him, time does not exist. He is not conscious of the passing of time, nor of the continuity of events; he lives in a world where past is indistinguishable from present. Old Man Compson believes that even Ben is aware of "the sequence of natural events and their causes which shadows every mans brow." This is true to the extent that Ben unconsciously manages to keep the time sequence of an incident straight in his memory. But he never consciously relates cause and effect in a time relationship; when he burns his hand he says simply, "I put my hand out to where the fire had been. . . . My hand jerked back and I put it in my mouth." In Ben's world, sensation is

dominant; everything is momentary, fleeting. Because Ben is un-
aware of the lapse of time, he is always approaching, but never
quite reaching, a pure specious present.

His lack of a concept of time is consistent with the other qualities
of his mind, and the combination of these qualities allows Faulkner
certain peculiar advantages in the structural sense. Because everything happens in the present for Ben, everything appears to him
in dramatic terms. And because there is no past for Ben, Faulkner
can give us a timeless view of the Compsons; he can cover the
whole range of the action and look forward to all the incidents
that are to follow. Furthermore, Ben's timeless view places the
Compsons outside historical time. One of the functions of Dilsey's
section is to put the downfall of the family into its historical context; thus, we see the family first in a situation opposite to that in
which we see them finally.

The dislocations of the time sequence within Ben's section are
natural functions of his mind, and it is these dislocations, brought
about by Ben's lack of a time sense, that cause him to make ironic
misinterpretations. Hearing the golfers call "caddie" in 1928, he
thinks they, too, are seeking his sister Caddy, whom he lost in
1910. If the circumstances surrounding any two acts are similar,
the two acts tend to merge in Ben's mind into one act; thus he
confuses his grandmother's funeral, which occurred in 1899, with
Caddy's wedding, which took place in 1910. Because he found
Caddy in the lawn swing with a man in 1908, when he finds Caddy's
daughter Quentin in the lawn swing twenty years later, he confuses
the two events. They become one event for him, and in some ways
the two women become for him one woman. Ben approaches, quite
ironically, that timeless state which Quentin, in his section, struggles
so hard to achieve.

If Ben is unconscious of time, Quentin is obsessed with it. . . .
Quentin's thoughts about time are derived from his father's
thoughts, as is much of his general philosophy. Essentially, Old
Man Compson thinks of time as he thinks of everything else—as
contradictory. Quentin says, "Father said clocks slay time. He said
time is dead as long as it is being clicked off by little wheels; only
when the clock stops does time come to life." But Quentin has
certain desires concerning time which are quite different from his
father's. It is important to see just what Quentin means when he
says, "and then I was in time again." Quentin wants to get outside
of time; he thinks of sleep as a temporary getting outside of it,
and he thinks of death as a permanent getting outside of it. We

only discover his reasons for this desire as we approach the end of his section. First, he wants to escape time because he knows that passing time will blunt his intense pain over Caddy, and he does not want that to happen. His second reason for wanting to forget time is paradoxical. He has decided that one way to get outside of time is to kill himself, and he has set a time for his suicide. But if he can manage in some way to *forget* time before the appointed hour, everything will be all right. Unless he does manage to forget time, time will keep moving forward inexorably, the appointed hour of his death will arrive, and he will have to kill himself in order to forget time. This is the reason for Quentin's struggle, throughout his section, against finding out what time it is. Here, as in the rest of that section, Faulkner has done an extraordinary job of representing the inverted logic of the suicide.

All day long Quentin tries various dodges in his attempt to forget time. Though he breaks his watch, the watch continues to tick, and time keeps on going, and he finds he can escape neither time's passing nor his coming death. The watch has a further symbolic value as well; it has been passed down from his forefathers. Not only does it shadow again the larger progression in historical time which Faulkner is trying to suggest, but it also marks a difference between Quentin's attitude toward time and his forefathers' attitude toward time. The watch, though marking only mechanical time, is tempered by humanity and enriched by history because it can be passed on as a token from one generation to the next. Quentin cannot tolerate the watch; his ancestors not only tolerated it, but valued it as a symbol.

If Quentin can sometimes forget mechanical time (as symbolized by clocks), he cannot forget those natural phenomena which mark off spaces in time. The sun's movement and shadows cast by the sun occupy his thoughts throughout his day. When he walks through the woods late in the afternoon, there appears again the characteristic inversion of Quentin's logic. "As I descended the light dwindled slowly, yet at the same time without altering its quality, as if I and not light were changing, decreasing."

But natural and mechanical time may both be subsumed under the classification "temporal": There is a more basic opposition which Quentin's mind mirrors—the opposition between "temporal" and "eternal." What Quentin really wants is to get outside of time, to get into eternity. "Eternal" implies a state in which change and motion are transcended; that is, an infinitely prolonged specious present. And it is this state which Quentin wishes to achieve. Such a concept of time is perfectly consistent with the dominant quality of Quentin's mind, emotion, or passion. Essentially, he tries all day to prepare himself for a mystical experience of the Absolute in which the contradictions of time and space are transcended. He attempts to whip himself up to an emotional trance, as it were.

His experience in the jeweler's shop reflects nearly all of his attitudes toward time. He manages to get past the shop at first by looking away quickly, but then he sees a clock "high up in the sun." That forces him to think of time again, and he returns to the shop. He uses his own broken watch as a pretext to ask the jeweler if "any of those watches in the window are right?" The jeweler thinks he wants to know what time it is and tries to tell him, but Quentin interrupts. "Don't tell me," he says, "please sir. Just tell me if any of them are right."

The jeweler ultimately gives him the answer he wants to hear— that none of the watches is correct. He wants to believe that watches lie, that they measure only apparent time, the opposite of real time. If there is only apparent time in the world, he may be able to get into real time without killing himself. But again he cannot escape, and the jeweler's shop becomes for him representative of the world, which is filled with the false ticking of clocks "like crickets in September grass" (natural and mechanical time are here joined once more). Only by leaving the shop can he escape false time. "I went out," he says, "shutting the door upon the ticking." Since he continually refers to death as a door, a perfect parallel is drawn: going out the door of the shop to get away from the ticking is like going out the door of death in order to escape time.

There are literally hundreds of cross references to time in Quentin's section; it is quite impossible even to list them all here. One or two instances are enough to illustrate the many forms of his obsession. The time of clock-hands holds all that Quentin wants to escape; the hands of the clock in the jeweler's window were "extended, slightly off the horizontal at a faint angle, like a gull tilting into the wind. Holding all I used to be sorry about like the new moon holding water, niggers say." When Quentin watches a schooner later, he sees gulls, and they bring up another relationship, the relation of time to space. There are three gulls near the schooner, "hovering above the stern like toys on invisible wires." And a little later he thinks,

Father said a man is the sum of his misfortunes. One day you'd think misfortune would get tired, but then time is your misfortune

Father said. A gull on an invisible wire attached through space dragged. You carry the symbol of your frustration into eternity.

It is noon by this time, and Quentin adds,

> I could hear my watch whenever the car stopped, but not often they were already eating. . . . Eating the buisness of eating inside of you space to space and time confused.

If he can just escape; if he can just be like the gulls hanging in static relation to the schooner, outside time and space, fixed and eternal, his problems will be solved. This is essentially the same idea that prompted him to tell his father that he and Caddy had committed incest so that they might be eternally isolated together in Hell.

Frequently he attempts to think of himself as already dead, or to remind himself that he will soon be dead. He can hardly think of the future; when he does, he immediately starts to use a jumble of verbs in the past tense. And he is continually changing present tenses into past tenses, especially when he uses the verb "to be." Sometimes there is an ironic confusion in his mind about past and present which is not unlike that in Ben's mind, and there is always an ironic mixture of the normal and the abnormal. He and the little Italian girl—who reminds him of Caddy—are walking by the river and come upon some boys swimming. This is the same river in which Quentin is to drown himself later in the evening. "Hear them in swimming, sister?" Quentin says, "I wouldn't mind doing that myself." And then he thinks, "If I had time. When I have time."

If Quentin's concept of time is central to his characterization, it also serves structure. His almost insane obsession with the relationship of time past and time present allows Faulkner to cut back and forth across the years 1899 to 1910 with a great deal of freedom; by using Quentin's time concept almost as an organizing principle, Faulkner can tell us all about Caddy's affairs, about the real relationship between Caddy and Quentin, and he can give an interpretation of all the family relationships hinted at in Ben's section. As we have seen, such knowledge is necessary if the reader is to understand the ironies and contradictions of Jason's section.

Jason is also obsessed with time, though in different manner and in slighter degree than is Quentin. All day long he rushes from place to place, but he never quite gets anywhere in time to accomplish his desires. Though he attempts to steal and hoard time just as he does money—and in a sense Jason thinks of time as money—he is always just a little too late. He "just misses" catching Miss Quentin and the man in the red tie; he is eternally late in getting cotton market reports; when the market falls, he finds out too late to save his capital. But his lateness is always self-induced; it is always a product of his almost frantic dashing about. Like a good many of Jason's doings, this tendency to be so busy saving time as never to have any becomes funny. At the end of this day, almost wild with frustration, he makes a last trip to the Western Union office and writes out a sardonic wire to his broker. The operator lets Jason write it out, and "then he looked at the clock. 'Market closed an hour ago,' he says."

Jason comes very close to the truth, though he does not realize it, when Miss Quentin asks him for money. "I haven't got any money," he says. "I've been too busy to make any." He is always telling someone he hasn't got time. "You'll have to go to the telegraph office and find that out," he says. "They'll have time to tell you. I haven't." There is a reverse side to this tendency in Jason as well. Because he himself steals and then wastes time, he suspects everyone else of stealing or wasting time, particularly Negroes. He accuses Old Job of taking time off to go to the tent-show, though he himself has been out chasing Miss Quentin; he accuses Dilsey of wasting time over lunch, though he himself is late for lunch; he fidgets while a Negro brings his car up, and says, quite characteristically, "After about a week he got back with it."

Thus, Jason never thinks of time as a continuum, but always in a mechanical and minute-to-minute sense. He has a fatalistic attitude toward time, as well; he always knows that "it's only a question of time," or he "knew all the time" that something was going to happen. Because time represents money to him, he has a tendency to measure time in terms of the first and last of the month; the times when bills come due and money comes in. Unlike Quentin, he does not believe watches lie, but quite the contrary; men lie, but watches, because they are mechanical devices, are to be trusted. When his boss, Earl, checks his watch against the town clock, Jason says, "You ought to have a dollar watch. It won't cost you so much to believe its lying every time."

Jason's view of time is consistent with his general mental attitude. His dominant faculty is reason, but because his reason is never tempered by sensation or emotion, he always comes to wrong conclusions. His mechanical view of time is a concept as false as either Ben's or Quentin's, though at the opposite extreme from theirs. His misunderstanding of the nature of time and his always being rushed and a little too late are symptoms of those traits in Jason which make it impossible for him to live well in his world. Jason's concept of time does less for the structure of the novel than Ben's or Quentin's. It allows Faulkner to emphasize the present, something which is desirable at this point, but primarily, it simply serves to characterize Jason.

It is when we begin to consider Dilsey's concept of time, however, that the real contrast to the time concepts held by the three Compson sons appears. Dilsey is aware of time, and aware of it in what might be called the "correct way." She is neither obsessed with time, as Jason and Quentin are, nor is she insensible of it, as Ben is. Whereas Jason tends to think of time only as something concrete, something to be used, and Quentin tends to think of time as an abstraction, Dilsey thinks of time in both senses.

Her first reference to time is an interesting one, because it involves the lying of a clock, something which both Quentin's and Jason's sections contain. And in certain respects the clock is startlingly similar to Quentin's broken watch. But Dilsey takes the clock's incorrectness as a matter of fact, and corrects for it automatically.

> On the wall above a cupboard, invisible save at night, by lamp light and even then evincing an enigmatic profundity because it had but one hand, a cabinet clock ticked, then with a preliminary sound as if it had cleared its throat, struck five times.
> "Eight oclock," Dilsey said.

The kitchen clock does not obtrude, then, as Quentin's loud-ticking watch did; whereas Quentin's watch had no hands, Dilsey's has one hand; when it lies, Dilsey knows by how much it lies.

And because Dilsey regards time correctly, she manages to accomplish those things which are necessary during the morning. Chaos breaks out around her, yet she finds time for everything, and even gets to church on time. Whereas clocks contribute to disorder in Quentin's and Jason's worlds, in Dilsey's kitchen the clock reflects order and peace.

> Then there was no sound in the kitchen save the simmering murmur of the kettle and the clock.
> . . . The clock tick-tocked, solemn and profound. It might have been the dry pulse of the decaying house itself; after a while it whirred and cleared its throat and struck six times.

On the practical plane, Dilsey's sensible attitude of accepting things as they occur allows her to operate successfully in her world. This attitude is summed up in her answer to Luster's question. "Is we gwine to church?" Luster asks. "I let you know bout dat when de time come," Dilsey says. But her attitude toward time is not merely practical. She has, as well, a proper understanding of the continuum of time, and for her eternity is an easy concept. When the Reverend Shegog begins the emotional part of his sermon, he launches into his theme by reminding the congregation that all generations pass away.

> Dey passed away in Egypt, de swingin chariots; de generations passed away. Wus a rich man: what he now, O breddren? Was a po man: what he now, O sistuhn? Oh I tells you, ef you aint got de milk en de dew of de old salvation when de long, cold years rolls away!

As he continues, Dilsey's thoughts run to Christ's birth and death and resurrection; for her, these events are so vivid as to be of the present. And because she grasps these ideas about the long reaches of time, she begins to think of the Compsons, who occupy so brief a place in history.

> "I've seed de first en de last," Dilsey said. . . .
> "First en last whut?" Frony said.
> "Never you mind," Dilsey said. "I seed de beginnin, en now I sees de endin."

Dilsey, then, realizes what has happened to the Compsons, and she sees them in their proper historical perspective. In her mind there is an interaction of all the faculties; sensation and emotion and reason work together, and this interaction allows her to understand time in its several senses. The opposition between temporal and eternal fades away, so far as Dilsey is concerned, when she lives by religion, and because it does, she sees the history of the Compsons properly. When she returns to her kitchen and once again hears the clock, the practical and the abstract senses of time merge.

> While she stood there the clock above the cupboard struck ten times. "One oclock," she said aloud, "Jason aint comin home. Ise seed de first en de last," she said, looking at the cold stove, "I seed de first en de last."

Dilsey's concept of time, then, serves structure as well as theme. Through her eyes the reader sees the Compson family in the proper historical perspective, which a correct time-sense gives. And her concept of time is put into direct contrast to both Jason's and Ben's in the final section. Ben's wailing, which "might have been all time and injustice and sorrow become vocal for an instant by a conjunction of planets," is set against Dilsey's thoughts as she sits stroking Ben's head and says, "Dis long time, O Jesus, dis long time." And while Dilsey is thinking of how Christ's birth and the present and eternity are all related in time, Jason, through his compulsion of haste, has come to the end of his rope in Mottson, and has become "a man sitting quietly behind the wheel of a small car, with his invisible life ravelled out about him like a worn-out sock." It is with Dilsey's section that the keystone to the arch of the whole book is dropped into place.

The Sound and the Fury is not a philosophical presentation of time concepts. Considered in context, time concepts and time devices work as integrating factors, factors which help the artist impose upon his material a form at once organic and effective and final.

Man, Time, and Eternity

by Cleanth Brooks

The salient technical feature of *The Sound and the Fury* is the use of four different points of view in the presentation of the breakup of the Compson family. . . . The reader's movement through the book is a progression from murkiness to increasing enlightenment, and this is natural, since we start with the mind of an idiot, go on next through the memories and reveries of the Hamlet-like Quentin, and come finally to the observations of the brittle, would-be rationalist Jason. Part of the sense of enlightenment comes simply from the fact that we are traversing the same territory in circling movements, and the cumulative effect of names and characterizations begins to dramatize for us with compelling urgency a situation we have come to accept almost as our own. . . . We do learn what it is like to live in such a family through being forced to share the minds of the three brothers in their special kinds of obsession. The sense of frustration and "entrapment" is overpowering. . . .

The states of consciousness of the three brothers provide three quite different modes of interpretation. Consider them, for a moment, under the rubric of poetry. Benjy's section is filled with a kind of primitive poetry, a poetry of the senses, rendered with great immediacy, in which the world—for Benjy a kind of confused, blooming buzz—registers with great sensory impact but with minimal intelligibility. Quentin's section is filled with poetry too, though his is essentially decadent: sensitive but neurotic and hopeless, as it rings sadly through a series of dying falls. Entering

"*Man, Time, and Eternity*," by *Cleanth Brooks. From* William Faulkner: The Yoknapatawpha Country (*New Haven: Yale University Press, 1963*), *Chap. 15. Copyright © 1963 by Yale University Press. Condensed and reprinted with permission from the publisher. The original essay includes a fuller discussion of all the major characters in the novel. Especially notable are Brooks' discussions of Quentin (the son) as "a classic instance of the courtly lover," of Quentin (the girl) as a symbol of the final disintegration of the Compson family, and of the relevance of the title's* Macbeth *allusion to the book's themes.*

Jason's section, we have no poetry at all, since Jason, the "sane" man, has consciously purged his mind of every trace of this perilous and impractical stuff. (One might claim, to be sure, that Jason's section does in fact attain to poetry, since perfect expression is in itself a kind of poetry. Jason's brilliant, if unconscious, parade of his vulgarity and his relentless exposure of his essential viciousness do carry prose—though ordinary and unpretentious—to the very brink of poetry.) With the last section we again encounter poetry, but of a more usual kind, especially in those passages which reveal Dilsey's reaction to the Easter service; and here it is neither primitive nor decadent, but whole, complex, and mature.

We can look at the four sections in quite another way, noticing what different conceptions of love they imply. Benjy represents love in its most simple and childlike form. His love for Caddy is intense and unreflective. . . . Quentin's love for Caddy is self-conscious, formal, even abstract. . . . He is not really in love with his sister's body, only in love with a notion of virginity that he associates with her. . . . In contrast with this incestuously Platonic lover, Jason has no love for Caddy at all, and no love for anyone else. . . . The relationship he desires is a commercial one: you know where you stand; there is no romantic nonsense about it. Jason, if he could, would reduce all relationships to commercial transactions.

Another way in which to contrast the first three sections is to observe the different notions of time held by the Compson brothers. Perrin Lowrey finds that each of the brothers has a defective sense of time. . . . Jean-Paul Sartre has argued, in an essay that has proved most influential, that Faulkner's characters, because they are committed to the past, are helpless. The Faulknerian character's point of view, as Sartre described it in a graphic metaphor, is that of a passenger looking backward from a speeding car, who sees, flowing away from him, the landscape he is traversing. For him the future is not in view, the present is too blurred to make out, and he can see clearly only the past as it streams away before his obsessed and backward-looking gaze. Sartre's account of the matter does apply in good measure to Quentin, but it does not apply to many of Faulkner's characters and it is certainly not to be attributed to Faulkner himself. Perhaps a more accurate way of stating the truth that inheres in Sartre's view is to say: man's very freedom is bound up with his sense of having some kind of future. Unless he can look ahead to the future, he is not free. The relation that the three Compson brothers bear to the future and to time in general has everything to do, therefore, with their status as human beings. Benjy . . . is locked almost completely into a timeless present. He has not much more sense of time than an animal has, and therefore he possesses not much more freedom than an animal does. . . . Quentin's obsession with the past is in fact a repudiation of the future. It amounts to the sense of having no future. . . . Jason, by insisting on seeing time only with regard to something to be done, is incapable of any real living. . . . Jason is so committed to preparation for the future that he is almost as enslaved as are his brothers.

. . . To Dilsey neither the past nor the future nor the present is oppressive, because to her they are all aspects of eternity, and her ultimate commitment is to eternity. It may be useful therefore to notice how the plight of each of the brothers constitutes a false interpretation of eternity. Benjy lives in a specious eternity: his present does not include all in timelessness—past, present, and future gathered together in a total pattern—but is a purely negative eternity, since it contains no past and no future. Quentin, we may say, wants to take eternity by storm—to reach it by a sort of shortcut, which in effect means freezing into permanence one fleeting moment of the past. Eternity is thus for Quentin not something which fulfills and enfolds all time, but simply a particular segment of time, like one note of music infinitely sustained. Jason is committed neither to a timeless present nor to a frozen past but to a making ready for the truly happy state. Jason's eternity is the empty mirage of an oasis toward which he is constantly flogging his tired camel and his tired self.

Though these patternings do emerge from a contemplation of the first three sections, and though they are important for an understanding of the novel, they do not show on the surface. The reader's impression of *The Sound and the Fury* is not of an elaborately formal abstract structure but quite the reverse. Rarely has a novel appeared so completely disordered and unconnected and accidental in its concreteness. . . . The patterns are there, but the knowledge that they are there is bought too dearly if it results in turning the three brothers into abstractions, mere stages in a dialectic. Quentin, for example, is a human being who, in spite of his anguished speculations upon the nature of time, is related to a culture; he is not a monstrous abstraction but a young man who has received a grievous psychic wound.

A way of seeing Quentin in a different, and perhaps a fuller, perspective is to note that he is another of Faulkner's many Puri-

tans. . . . Quentin reveals his Puritanism most obviously in his
alarm at the breakdown of sexual morality. When the standards of
sexual morality are challenged, a common reaction and one quite
natural to Puritanism is to try to define some point beyond which
surely no one would venture to transgress—to find at least one act
so horrible that everyone would be repelled by it. . . .

Whatever the special causes of Quentin's spiritual malaise, the
general conditioning cause is quite evident. The curse upon
Quentin and the rest of the Compsons is the presence of their
hypochondriac, whining mother. Again and again on his last day
of life he says to himself, "If I only had a mother," and he remembers associating his mother with a scene pictured in one of the books
in the family library. There was portrayed "a dark place into
which a single weak ray of light came slanting upon two faces
lifted out of the shadow" (p. 191). In Quentin's troubled memory
the pictured faces become those of his mother and father. He remembers that he would feel a compulsion to turn back to the
picture until "the dungeon was Mother herself she and Father upward into weak light holding hands and us lost somewhere below
even them without even a ray of light." Remembering his mother
on the day of his death, Quentin says to himself: "Done in Mother's
mind though. Finished. Finished. Then we were all poisoned"
(p. 121).

The Sound and the Fury has on occasion been read as another
Faulknerian document describing the fall of the Old South. Perhaps it is, but what it most clearly records is the downfall of a
particular family, and the case seems rather special. The basic cause
of the breakup of the Compson family—let the more general cultural causes be what they may—is the cold and self-centered mother
who is sensitive about the social status of her own family, the Bascombs, who feels the birth of an idiot son as a kind of personal
affront, who spoils and corrupts her favorite son, and who with-
holds any real love and affection from her other children and her
husband. Caroline Compson is not so much an actively wicked
and evil person as a cold weight of negativity which paralyzes the
normal family relationships. She is certainly at the root of Quentin's lack of confidence in himself and his inverted pride. She is
at least the immediate cause of her husband's breakdown into alcoholic cynicism, and doubtless she is ultimately responsible for
Caddy's promiscuity. . . .

Mr. Compson by 1910 was a defeated man. Perhaps he had always
been a weak man, not endowed with the fighting spirit necessary to

save his family. But there are plenty of indications that he was a man possessed of love and compassion. . . . Evidently, the knowledge of his daughter's wantonness had hit Mr. Compson hard, and his parade of cynicism about women and virginity, so much of which Quentin recalls on the day of his death, must have been in part an attempt to soften the blow for Quentin and perhaps for himself. We miss the point badly if we take it that Mr. Compson, comfortable in his cynicism, simply didn't care what his daughter did.

Quentin was apparently very close to his father and the influence of his father on him was obviously very powerful. The whole of the Quentin section is saturated with what "Father said" and with references to comparisons that Father used and observations about life that Father made. Though his father seems to have counseled acquiescence in the meaninglessness of existence, it is plain that it was from him that Quentin derived his high notion of the claims of honor. . . . Quentin is emotionally committed to the code of honor, but for him the code has lost its connection with reality: it is abstract, rigidified, even "literary." Quentin's suicide results from the fact that he can neither repudiate nor fulfill the claims of the code. . . .

The third brother, Jason, has repudiated the code of honor. He has adopted for himself a purely practical formula for conduct. Money is what counts. . . . But though Jason's ostensible code is purely practical, reducing every action to its cash value, his conduct has in fact its nonpractical aspect. For Jason harbors a great deal of nonpractical and irrational bitterness, even sadism. . . . Sanity as Jason exemplifies it is something inhuman. Jason does not love even his mother, Faulkner tells us, for he is "a sane man always," and love always involves a contradiction of such sanity. Benjy's idiocy and Quentin's quixotic madness are finally less inhuman than Jason's sanity. To be truly human one must transcend one's mere intellect with some overflow of generosity and love. Faulkner tells us that Jason is able to compete with, and even hold his own with, the Snopeses. This is the highest accolade that Faulkner can bestow on Jason, and of course, the worst damnation that he can utter. When a Compson turns Snopes, then the family has indeed run out, and the end of an order has come.

The section devoted to Jason has in it some of the most brilliant writing that Faulkner ever did. . . . Faulkner does more in these eighty pages to indict the shabby small-town businessman's view of life than Sinclair Lewis was able to achieve in several novels on the subject. Jason takes his place as one of the half-dozen of Faulkner's most accomplished villains. . . . A common trait in Faulkner's villains is the lack of any capacity for love. Their lack of love shows itself in two ways, two ways that come eventually to the same thing: their attitudes toward nature and toward women. They do not respond to nature—they may very well violate nature. In quite the same way, they have no interest in women, or use them as means to their own ends. . . . Jason Compson, with no interest in nature, or in women except as objects to be manipulated, is of this breed. . . .

The downfall of the house of Compson is the kind of degeneration which can occur, and has occurred, anywhere at any time. The real significance of the Southern setting in *The Sound and the Fury* resides, as so often elsewhere in Faulkner, in the fact that the breakdown of a family can be exhibited more poignantly and significantly in a society which is old-fashioned and in which the family is still at the center. The dissolution of the family as an institution has probably gone further in the suburban areas of California and Connecticut than it has in the small towns of Mississippi. For that very reason, what happens to the Compsons might make less noise and cause less comment, and even bring less pain to the individuals concerned, if the Compsons lived in a more progressive and liberal environment. Because the Compsons have been committed to old-fashioned ideals—close family loyalty, home care for defective children, and the virginity of unmarried daughters—the breakup of the family registers with greater impact.

The decay of the Compsons can be viewed, however, not merely with reference to the Southern past but to the contemporary American scene. It is tempting to read it as a parable of the disintegration of modern man. Individuals no longer sustained by familial and cultural unity are alienated and lost in private worlds. One thinks here not merely of Caddy, homeless, the sexual adventuress adrift in the world, or of Quentin, out of touch with reality and moving inevitably to his death, but also and even primarily of Jason, for whom the breakup of the family means an active rejection of claims and responsibilities and, with it, a sense of liberation. . . .

The one member of the Compson household who represents a unifying and sustaining force is the Negro servant Dilsey. . . . Faulkner does not present Dilsey as a black fairy-godmother or as a kind of middle-aged Pollyanna full of the spirit of cheerful optimism. Even his physical description of her looks in another direction. We are told that she had once been a big woman, but now the unpadded skin is loosely draped upon "the indomitable skeleton" which is left "rising like a ruin or a landmark above the somnolent and impervious guts, and above that the collapsed face that gave the impression of the bones themselves being outside the flesh, lifted into the driving day with an expression at once fatalistic and of a child's astonished disappointment" (p. 282). What the expression means is best interpreted by what she says and does in the novel, but the description clearly points to something other than mindless cheeriness. Dilsey's essential hopefulness has not been obliterated; she is not an embittered woman, but her optimism has been chastened by hurt and disappointment.

Faulkner does not make the mistake of accounting for Dilsey's virtues through some mystique of race in which good primitive black folk stand over against corrupt wicked white folk. Dilsey herself has no such notions. When her son Luster remarks of the Compson household: "Dese is funny folks. Glad I aint none of em," she says: "Lemme tell you somethin, nigger boy, you got jes es much Compson devilment in you es any of em" (p. 292). She believes in something like original sin: men are not "naturally" good but require discipline and grace.

Dilsey, then, is no noble savage and no *schöne Seele*. Her view of the world and mankind is thoroughly Christian, simple and limited as her theological expression of her faith would have to be. On the other hand, Dilsey is no plaster saint. She is not easy on her own children. ("Dont stand dar in de rain, fool," she tells Luster.) She does not always offer the soft answer that turneth away wrath. She rebukes Mrs. Compson with "I dont see how you expect anybody to sleep, wid you standin in de hall, holl'in at folks fum de crack of dawn," and she refuses Mrs. Compson's hypocritical offer to fix breakfast, saying: "En who gwine eat yo messin? Tell me dat" (p. 287). Dilsey's goodness is no mere goodness by, and of, nature, if one means by this a goodness that justifies a faith in man as man. Dilsey does not believe in man; she believes in God.

Dilsey's poverty and her status as a member of a deprived race do not, then, assure her nobility, but they may have had something to do with her remaining close to a concrete world of values so that she is less perverted by abstraction and more honest than are most white people in recognizing what is essential and basic. In general, Faulkner's Negro characters show less false pride, less false idealism, and more seasoned discipline in human relationships. Dilsey's race has also had something to do with keeping her close to a world still informed by religion. These matters are important: just how important they are is revealed by the emphasis Faulkner gives to the Easter service that Dilsey attends.

The Compson family—whatever may be true of the white community at large in the Jefferson of 1910—has lost its religion. Quentin's sad reveries are filled with references to Jesus and Saint Francis, but it is plain that he has retreated into some kind of Stoicism, a version which is reflected in his father's advice to him: "We must just stay awake and see evil done for a little." Quentin's reply is that "it doesn't have to be even that long for a man of courage" (p. 195), and the act of courage in the Roman style takes Quentin into the river. Mrs. Compson, when she finds that the girl Quentin has eloped, asks Dilsey to bring her the Bible, but obviously Mrs. Compson knows nothing about either sin or redemption. Her deepest concern is with gentility and social position. And Jason, as we have seen, worships only the almighty dollar.

Christian and Freudian Structures

by Carvel Collins

Most readers of *The Sound and the Fury* have been aware ever since its publication in 1929 that three of its four sections are set on Easter Sunday and the two days preceding it, and that the dates of these three days appear as the section headings. . . . The date of Quentin Compson's monologue turns out to fall on a Thursday so that even though it is in 1910 rather than the 1928 of the other three carefully dated sections, it makes Quentin's section form with them a sequence of Thursday, Friday, Saturday, and Sunday. And Quentin's monologue, bearing this Thursday date, contains the elements of Christ's experience on Holy Thursday. The parallel with the Bible and liturgy is rich in detail, and here I should like to list a few of the points of similarity: Quentin has a Last Supper not only when he joins Shreve and Gerald and their companions in the picnic with its wine (and blood) but when he "breaks bread" with the little Italian girl in a parallel with the establishment of the Eucharist and its later ritual, even including Holy Thursday's presanctification of the Host. Quentin's tortured conversation with his father is an important part of his memories during this monologue which takes place on the same day of the week as Christ's anguished calling upon His Father. Quentin is captured by a mob as Christ was. And, like Christ, he is taken before a magistrate.[1]

"Christian and Freudian Structures," [Editor's title,] by Carvel Collins. From "The Pairing of The Sound and the Fury and As I Lay Dying," The Princeton University Library Chronicle, XVIII (Spring, 1957), 115-19. Copyright © 1957, by the Princeton University Library. Reprinted with permission from the author and the publisher.

[1] In a letter to the editor, Professor Collins has extended this argument as follows: "The date at the head of Quentin's monologue is the date of the Octave of Corpus Christi in 1910, and Corpus Christi is Holy Thursday reenacted in a happier context at another time of year and with the addition of new elements, one of them the carrying of the bread through the streets (cf. Quentin and the little Italian girl with her loaf)."

Jason's section, bearing the date of Good Friday, 1928, shows this Compson son going through events symbolically parallel with those Christ was involved in on the Friday of His Passion. Good Friday is a day on which Christ's mother was closely associated with his suffering: Mrs. Compson—not the father as in Quentin's section—appears at length in this monologue, which also has its Magdalen in Jason's Memphis friend. Jason's name seems significant, for though it has been said to relate him to the seeker of the Golden Fleece it was also used for "Jesus" by Hellenized Jews. Christ went upon the Cross at noon of this day and died there at three o'clock: Jason, being commercially crucified, enters cotton speculation at noon and is sold out of the market by his Jewish brokers at three. Christ's soul went to harrow Hell: when Jason tells his niece to go to Hell she replies that she will, and after his commercial crucifixion is over at three he leaves town chasing her and her circus companion whose red necktie Jason says he will make Hell's latchstring. . . .

The monologue of Benjamin Compson, the idiot, bears the date of Holy Saturday, 1928. Robert M. Adams correctly says that tradition holds that Christ spent Holy Saturday in Hell redeeming such pre-Christian worthies as Adam, and that in this monologue we are sunk in the mind of the idiot Benjy.[2] But his opinion that Benjy is Adam and that the young attendant of Benjy is Christ seems to be in error. Instead, Benjy, like his brothers in the other two monologues, is going through the events Christ went through on a particular day of His Passion. Benjy's birthday candles are reminiscent of the paschal candle which is a large feature of church ritual on Holy Saturday. Fire fascinates Benjy on this day of ritualistic lighting of the new fire. On this traditional day of christening there is considerable ado about the naming of Benjy. And Benjy's tormenting young attendant is certainly an agent of Hell.

In the novel's fourth section, bearing the date of Easter Sunday, 1928, the events involving the Compson family are parallel with those involving Christ on Easter. As one example: Miss Quentin's empty room and abandoned lingerie have pointed relationship with Christ's empty tomb and discarded grave clothes.

There was a time when people presented with this opinion that the structure of *The Sound and the Fury* is in close and sustained

² Robert M. Adams, "Poetry in the Novel: or, Faulkner Esemplastic," *Virginia Quarterly Review*, XXIX (Summer, 1953), 419-434. See also Sumner C. Powell, "William Faulkner Celebrates Easter, 1928," *Perspective*, II (Summer, 1949), 195-218.

parallel with the Passion would reply that, though Mr. Faulkner might once have made considerable use of such a parallel in creating the character and circumstances of Joe Christmas in *Light in August,* it was inconceivable that he would carry a parallel of this sort to such lengths as I believed he had in *The Sound and the Fury.* But that was before the appearance in 1954 of *A Fable,* with its close, sustained, and obvious parallel between the French pacifist soldier and the Prince of Peace.

Examination of these motifs in *The Sound and the Fury* and the array of details which cannot be presented here make clear that the Compson sons are in parallel with Christ but, significantly, by inversion. For example, Christ pleaded to be released from the next day's torture if such release would not interfere with His Father's plans, but Quentin pleads with his father for punishment —which is refused him. When Benjamin is submerged like Christ on Holy Saturday, he does not, like Christ, dominate Hell; on the contrary, he is a victim of it. And whereas Holy Saturday is a time of christening, of name giving, an important fact about Benjy which is presented in his monologue on Holy Saturday is that *his* name has been taken away. In short, God's Son passed through the events of the Passion and rose as a redeemer; the Compson sons pass through parallel events but go down in failure. And they do so because love, which Christ preached as an eleventh commandment, is lacking or frustrated or distorted in their family. The major theme of the novel is not the sociology of a section of the South but the psychology of certain aspects of human life wherever found.

This interpretation of *The Sound and the Fury* is bolstered by another structural system in the novel. One problem of part of the novel's Christian parallel is that all three Compson sons appear in parallel with Jesus, when a single figure running through the whole parallel would have made for a more easily apprehended unity. But it seems to me that the three Compsons merge at a symbolic level into what is, in a sense, a single figure: Benjamin lives and operates at the level of the primitive and inarticulate id as Freud described it; Quentin at that of the ego, which Freud presented as a battleground between the urges of the id and the restraints of the super-ego; and Jason at that of the repressive super-ego. Thus, though the wonderfully unbroken surface story of the novel shows these three Southern men to be separate brothers believably and concretely involved in realistic events, a hidden and abstract level merges them for certain purposes into one personality. For example,

Benjamin (who, like the id as Freud described it, has no sense whatever of time or sequence) goes to sleep at the end of his monologue; on the next page, in the first sentence of the next son's monologue, Quentin wakes saying (in keeping with Freud's description of the ego as the first part of the personality to become aware of time), "Then I was in time again." [3] Whether Mr. Faulkner did or did not consciously put this second system into the novel, it is impossible to say. But one would like to think so, for to merge the three sons into one in this way helps not only to pull together the parallel with Christ but to elucidate further the theme of the effects of lack of love.

[3] Collins argues in much greater detail for the Freudian analogies in "The Interior Monologues of 'The Sound and the Fury,'" *English Institute Essays, 1952*, ed. Alan S. Downer (New York: Columbia University Press, 1954), pp. 29-56.

Quentin and the Walking Shadow:
The Dilemma of Nature and Culture

by Louise Dauner

In the Quentin section (Part II) of William Faulkner's *The Sound and the Fury*, the structure of Quentin's tragic experience is given by several repeated symbolic motifs. These include, by my count, and in the order of frequency, water (61 times), shadow (53), door (34), sister (30), honeysuckle (27), plus scattered references to time, as carried by Quentin's watch, the Harvard chimes, and various clocks. Since the action of the section culminates in Quentin's suicide by drowning, it is appropriate that water should be numerically the dominant motif, with its psychological and mythic implications as the unconscious, or the waters of death and rebirth, into which he escapes in a final ritualistic purification. The shadow-motif, however, though second in frequency, covers a greater variety of meanings than do the others. . . . Definition of the shadow-implications not only illuminates the complex character of Quentin, but provides insight into the total experience recorded in this section. . . .

The association which comes first to mind is metaphorical and philosophical. It is of course the echo derived from the title of the novel, which appears in Macbeth's soliloquy (Act V, scene v), after the death of Lady Macbeth. Pertinent lines are

> . . . Out, out brief candle!
> Life's but a walking shadow, a poor player,
> That struts and frets his hour upon the stage

And then is heard no more. It is a tale
Told by an idiot, full of sound and fury,
Signifying nothing . . .

"Life's but a walking shadow" elicits a further echo of the shadows
in Plato's Cave (*The Republic,* Book VII), the illusions which man
in his ignorance mistakes for reality. Without implying that Quentin's whole vision of life is unreal and without value in the America
of the early twentieth century, we may still see that Quentin is increasingly unable to distinguish life as it is from life as he would
have it, or as it seems to him to have been in a more chivalric and
aristocratic Southern past. He is a romantic, beset by the growing
crudities of a naturalistic culture. . . . Quentin can not accept
what his father once called "the sequence of natural events and
their causes which shadows every mans brow," that genesis of Evil
which lies in the heart of man, and of which one aspect is the
struggle between man's instinctual nature and all that man has
superimposed upon this and called culture. This dilemma of Nature and Culture is not peculiar to Quentin alone, but is a part of
the human condition. Quentin's father tells him, "It's nature is
hurting you not Caddy" (p. 135). On the other hand, Jung reminds
us that "man can suffer only a certain amount of culture without
injury." Quentin's life has lain under the shadow of this dilemma,
Nature being concretized in the lives of his family, and Culture in
the lingering concepts of a traditional Southern past. His own subjective values do not correlate with the objective world in which
he must live. . . .

In the first half of the section especially, the shadow frequently
functions as a literal time and space signal. But often a shadow
merges with an object or element which serves as a psychological
"springboard," associating in Quentin's mind with some aspect of
his obsession with Caddy. Thus, when the shadow of the sash moves
inside the door of Quentin's room, "driving the shadow back into
the door" (p. 100), Quentin remembers Caddy's wedding, Caddy
running through the door, and "the floating shadow of the veil"
(p. 101). In fact, often the shadow serves as the core of a cluster of
obsessive memories of Caddy. For example, "their shadows one
shadow her head rose it was above his on the sky higher their two
heads . . . then not two heads . . . we shook hands then we stood
there her shadow high against his shadow one shadow . . ." (p. 173).
Here Quentin recalls the episode when he and Caddy had contem-

plated his killing her and then himself, followed by Caddy's meeting with one of her lovers. The fusion of the two shadows bespeaks the constant sex-preoccupation of both Quentin and Caddy. Related to this aspect is Quentin's preoccupation with virginity (an oblique response, since Caddy is not virgin). "I thought about how I'd thought about I could not be a virgin, with so many of them walking along in the shadows and whispering with their soft girlvoices lingering in the shadowy places and the words coming out and perfume and eyes you could feel not see, but if it was that simple to do it wouldnt be anything and if it wasnt anything, what was I . . ." (p. 166). Here Quentin's torturing confusion about abstractions emphasizes his inability to accept concrete realities, and his insecurity and psychic disunity.

The largest group of shadow-implications, however, combines the sense of time, as the sun moves through the day, with the theme of self-punishment. In these instances, the shadow is Quentin's own shadow, which thus assumes meaning as the Double, the alter ego, the "dark brother." As Quentin gets on or off street cars, or moves into or out of the sunlight during this Via Doloroso of his last day, he loses his shadow or finds it again. (The leitmotiv of light and darkness is a constant backdrop for the action in this section). Or he plays a game with his shadow: "The wall went into shadow, and then my shadow, I had tricked it again" (p. 153). In such instances, the shadow assumes both a primitive and a sophisticated meaning, for it connects with both anthropology and folklore, and with analytical psychology. . . .

To summarize the anthropological aspects of the shadow, it is first the soul, the connoter of immortality. Second, as the immortal part, its injury or loss indicates illness or death. These implications are significant in regard to Quentin's shadow. . . . Many instances suggest his wish to injure or destroy his shadow. He takes a streetcar until he reaches water and a drawbridge where he gets off. There he crosses the bridge and leans over the rail. "The shadow of the bridge . . . my shadow leaning flat upon the water, so easily had I tricked it that it would not quit me. At least fifty feet it was, and if I only had something to blot it into the water, holding it until it was drowned . . . Niggers say a drowned man's shadow was watching for him in the water all the time" (p. 109). Again, later, he reflects, "When I can see my shadow again if not careful that I tricked into the water shall tread again upon my impervious shadow" (p. 114). During his afternoon's peregrinations, he returns frequently to the same theme. . . . The punishment theme bespeaks his neurotic compulsion to assume a guilt not his, as he had tried to convince his father that he had committed incest with Caddy. Here then the shadow functions both as the double-self, and, in its loss or abuse, as a foreshadowing (no pun intended) of Quentin's impending suicide; for the height of self-punishment is suicide.

Closely related to the aspect of the shadow as the opposing self is the Jungian Shadow archetype. . . . The Shadow is the repressed, excluded, inferior aspect of the psyche. . . . Quentin's desire for Caddy can logically be construed as the real basis for self-punishment and for his eventual suicide. Or again, his basic tension is that he denies his instinctual nature, which Caddy so intensely exemplifies, hence he denies his own shadow. . . . His encounter with the Shadow, which Jung calls "the apprentice-piece in the individual's development," is avoided or perverted, and is symbolized by his gestures of destroying the shadow, by tricking it, trampling upon it, or drowning it. His effort to escape his shadow is suggested when he speaks of "my shadow, pacing me, dragging its head through the weeds that hid the fence," as he tries to escape the little Italian girl (a sister proxy) who had fastened herself upon him. But the shadow is inescapable; and the connotation of its dragging its head through the weeds suggests the sense of shame and guilt which Quentin must bear with him wherever he goes. His failure to come to terms with his darker aspect (what Jung calls the integration with the Shadow) defines his psychic immaturity and disunity. Interpreted as an archetypal symbol, the shadow thus reveals much about Quentin's character and his real motives for suicide.

The above connotations of obsession, psychic disunity, and death seem to be caught up together in another of Quentin's memories of the mutual death pact. After the moment has passed, Caddy meets one of her lovers and Quentin goes off for a walk. A little later, Caddy comes along the bank. Quentin asks Caddy whether she loves this man now, and as she replies, "I don't know," he is aware in the gray light of "shadows of things like dead things in stagnant water" (p. 176). He tells her, "I wish you were dead." Here the shadows, in the context and in their generality, seem to include all of Quentin's basic obsessions—with Caddy, with sex, with death—as well as all that we sense by now of the deterioration of the family—"dead things"—the traditions and attributes of a once distinguished family, drowned in the "stagnant waters" of a heroic but now vanquished past and a decaying present.

Another instance in which the shadows carry a generalized negative implication occurs when Quentin, after his perambulatory day, is again on a streetcar on the way back to the Harvard quadrangle. It is twilight. The car passes the place where, that morning, he had last seen water. Now the water reminds him of the spring rains at home, and of his trying to put himself to sleep, until "after the honeysuckle got all mixed up in it the whole thing came to symbolize night and unrest I seemed to be lying neither asleep nor awake looking down a long corridor of grey halflight where all stable things had become shadowy paradoxical all I had done shadows all I had felt suffered taking visible form antic and perverse mocking without relevance inherent themselves with the denial of the significance they should have affirmed thinking I was I was not who was not was not who" (p. 188). Here the shadows suggest the totality of Quentin's experience—shadowy, paradoxical, perverse, sterile, unreal. From this memory of spiritual miasma he recalls a last dialogue with his father in which he rejects his father's rhetorical cynicism and suggests the possibility of his own suicide. He then gets off the streetcar, goes back to his room, sets himself and his belongings in order, and departs to enact the climax of his personal drama.

As a counterpoint to this accumulation of negative implications, there is, however, one situation in which the shadow appears to function positively. As Quentin is hanging over the rail of the bridge in the morning, he looks deep into the water:

> Where the shadow of the bridge fell I could see down for a long way but not as far as the bottom. When you leave a leaf in the water a long time after awhile the tissue will be gone and the delicate fibers waving slow as the motion of sleep. They dont touch one another, no matter how knotted up they once were, no matter how close they lay once to the bones. And maybe when He says Rise the eyes will come floating up too, out of the deep quiet and the sleep, to look on glory. . . .
>
> I could not see the bottom, but I could see a long way into the motion of the water before the eye gave out, and then I saw a shadow hanging like a flat arrow stemming into the current. . . . The arrow increased without motion, then in a quick swirl the trout lipped a fly beneath the surface. . . . The fading vortex drifted away down stream and then I saw the arrow again, now into the current, wavering delicately to the motion of the water. . . . The trout hung, delicate and motionless among the wavering shadows. Three boys with fishing poles came onto the bridge and we leaned on the rail and looked down at the trout. They knew the fish. He was a neighborhood character (pp. 135-36).

This trout bears some relationship to the legendary bear of Faulkner's short story "The Bear." Both fish and bear are of somewhat heroic proportions. Both are "characters" in their vicinities. And neither is to be caught or killed by any usual procedure. . . .

Just as Quentin sees the fish, he is thinking of death, of the disintegration of the body in water, and of the Resurrection of the dead. There is even a speculative note of redemption: "Maybe when He says Rise the eyes will come floating up too . . . to look on glory." An additional religious touch appears in the conjunction of the big trout with the three young fishermen. The redemptive religious note is invoked because the fish has for centuries been a Christian symbol. The Greek word for *fish* is *ichthys*, which is an anagram formed by the first letters of the Greek phrase which translates into English as Jesus Christ, Son of God, Savior. Into Quentin's thoughts of death, and his spiritually myopic vision ("I could see down for a long way but not as far as the bottom"), and on this "Maundy Thursday" with its Easter-burden of the sacrifice of the divine mediator, comes the great apparently immortal fish. . . .

The fish-shadow suggests itself then as a redemptive antidote or balance to the weight of Quentin's tragic experience, in which suicide is the climax. And let us not forget that suicide is the exact opposite of the self-sacrifice of Christ for humanity. Though the redemptive note is not followed up in any concrete way, it does provide one alleviating touch, one golden thread, in the dark fabric of Quentin's experience. Otherwise, though we do not see Quentin's death, by the end of the section we are back where we began, with "Out, out brief candle." . . . In its essential signification, the word *shadow* limns for us the illusory, fantasy-ridden world of Quentin Compson, for whom there is neither peace nor reality except in the all-embracing maternal waters of death. Here, if anywhere, he may at last be reconciled with his Shadow.

Quentin as Romantic

by Robert M. Slabey

Quentin's stream of consciousness is filled with allusions. He is, quite literally, sitting upon the shore, with the arid plain behind him, trying to set his life in order. These fragments from literature and history he would "shore" against the ruins. The number of likenesses which have been found between Quentin and other literary figures gives some indication of the rich texture of the novel. Quentin has been likened to Hamlet (the time is out of joint and he is unable to set it right; his melancholy, indecision, and obsession with the sexual sin in women); to Macbeth (the projection of his own inner chaos onto the world; the concept of life as empty, meaningless, futile, like "a walking shadow"); to Dante's Paolo (the desire to suffer eternally in hell with his lover, "beyond the clean flame"); to Raskolnikov (similar family relationships; concerned with his sister's virginity; unsteady, masochistic university student, planning murder, contemplating suicide by drowning); to Stephen Dedalus (alienated and attached to homeland, preoccupied with time, haunted with feelings of guilt); to Scott's Quentin Durward (Scottish ancestry, valuing honor in an age which has abandoned it); and to Prufrock ("sick," weak, spiritless, withdrawing from life, "not Prince Hamlet"). One distinctive feature to be found to some degree in each of these figures is the Romantic sensibility: all of them are clinging to an impossible ideal in the face of hard facts; all are egocentric, even narcissistic, trying to live in a private inner world of their own, in a way committing intellectual incest. . . .

The Romantic sensibility is a movement towards what Allen Tate calls "The Angelic Imagination" and what Father William Lynch calls "Manichaean Dissociation." . . . In Quentin there is

"*Quentin as Romantic,*" [*Editor's title,*] by *Robert M. Slabey. From "The 'Romanticism' of* The Sound and the Fury," *The Mississippi Quarterly, XVI (Summer, 1963), 152-57. Copyright © 1963 by Mississippi State University. Condensed and reprinted with permission from* The Mississippi Quarterly *and Robert M. Slabey.*

a Manichaean revulsion against the physical, the sexual, the limited, the temporal, a romantic repudiation of the immediate realities of human life, and a direction toward the infinite and the timeless. Quentin is obsessed with keeping his body pure from stain . . . ; in like manner, his suicide is a gesture against human contingency, a setting the spirit free from the pollution of the flesh. . . .

Quentin, in his desire to "eternalize" his grief, is again the Romantic. This desire is for the "eternal present" of Keats, the arrested action "out of time," the supreme moments immortalized on a Grecian urn. . . . Death becomes a "poetic" experience, an encounter with eternity in the present moment, the eternal imprisonment of a temporary ecstasy. The moment of death is the moment when time stops, when the present becomes past and the future does not exist. *Eros* and *thanatos* are inseparable. When the lover realizes that love cannot be fulfilled in life, he flees to death but still longs for an earthly answer to his desires. Again this is Quentin's story: the conflict between passion and reason, the ideal and the real, the movement away from the realm of actual experience, and the identification of love and death. Quentin is fastidious; his primping, washing himself, and brushing his clothes before his suicide resemble the actions of a man preparing to meet a lover. And Quentin is such a man: he is in love with death. . . .

Quentin would deny the shadow-part of his personality, the "underground" forces of life; he tries to appear better, more virtuous, and more rational than he really is. Ironically, the shadow, which he would repress, plays a large part in his downfall; much of the darkness which he finds in the exterior world is in reality a projection of his own diseased mind ("Life's but a walking shadow"). He does not recognize that part of the family's collapse is his own doing. Underneath the casual, futile, and sometimes chaotic events of June 2, 1910, the Shadow is steadily leading him to his death. Quentin never knows that the one thing he cannot escape is himself. His father had told him, "you are still blind to what is in yourself to that part of general truth the sequence of natural events and their causes which shadows every mans brow even benjys."

The Locus and Status of Meaning

by John W. Hunt

Two major themes run at counterpoint throughout *The Sound
and the Fury,* qualifying and deepening one another, neither emerg-
ing as unambiguously dominant and neither mitigated for the sake
of the other. . . . Both themes refer finally to the status of meaning in modern experience: the first to its negative status, loss and
absence; the second to its positive status, presence and endurance. . . . Benjy's section introduces both themes without giving
focus to either. Quentin strives to establish the reality of the second
but succeeds only in affirming the first. Though he assumes the
reality of the second theme, Jason, too, by the dramatic irony of
his section, affirms the negative status of meaning. Dilsey's section
brings both themes into focus, and the second emerges as dominant. . . .

. . . Quentin asks of life that it be meaningful in a certain way,
namely that it support what he takes to be the traditional criterion
of meaning. . . . His understanding of the tradition is purely
moralistic and intellectual. He does not participate in its spirit, but
has learned its forms, interpreting them with a legalistic rigidity
which precludes his bending to present experience and presages his
breaking against it.

As he develops his various strategies for dealing with present experience, he undergoes an intellectualization of his problem. . . .
For all the apparent disorganization of his section, it is possible to
discern three major phases through which his character has pro-
gressed: an initial focus upon Caddy's sexual behavior as the test
of the tradition's validity in the present; a shift in focus from

---

"The Locus and Status of Meaning," by John W. Hunt. From William
Faulkner: Art in Theological Tension *(Syracuse: Syracuse University Press,
1965), Chap. 2. Copyright 1965 by Syracuse University Press. Condensed and
reprinted with permission from the publisher. Hunt's sixty-page chapter is
by far the longest essay yet published on* The Sound and the Fury. *It includes,
among other things, a detailed analysis of Quentin's development from childhood and the fullest existing discussion of Jason.*

ethics to metaphysics, from sex to time as his private problem, with the added attempt here to bring sex and time together; and, finally, a capitulation to his father's nihilism, a concern with being itself, with death as a means of avoiding the meaninglessness of time by referring his problem to eternity. . . .

Quentin's report of the events of his last day—including the recollections of past events—should be read in the light of his third phase, his condition at the point of suicide. The precipitant, unsorted, and dreamlike character of his recollections is accounted for by the fact that he has reached the point where the past has completely pre-empted his consciousness. Present occurrences trigger recollections and take on a fixity as he relates them to his past. The complex symbolism of shadow, door, bird, slanting, clocks, honeysuckle, flowers, wistaria, water—in short, all the sounds, feelings, smells, and sights associated with what are in his consciousness the significant events of his life—reveals the content of all three phases. Each of the symbolic images compresses most of the others. In many of the passages of recollection, one image will evoke others or substitute for others. For example, honeysuckle, probably the most important single image, is associated with water or wetness (rain, drizzle, mist) since the smell of honeysuckle hangs heavily in the wet atmosphere of the crucial hog wallow and suicide compact scenes; it therefore also recalls images of sex and death, of shadow, twilight, greyness, of Benjy's bellowing, of Caddy's marriage, and of time and being. It suffuses his very breath of life: "I had to pant to get any air at all out of that thick grey honeysuckle" (170). Quentin's recapitulation of his life in the sensuous language of symbolic imagery serves at once to render the quality of his sensibility and to reveal the thematic contribution of his section to the novel as a whole.

An analysis of the symbolic imagery shows that Quentin's concern with the loss of meaning is extended to include his personal past. He despairs of preserving in time even the immediacy of his own sensitivity to the loss of meaning and in a last psychotic wrench of his intellect sees life's meaninglessness and emptiness solved by a negation of being itself. At the point of suicide he has completely subjected public reality to his private hurt.

External reality in the final stage is oblique, shaded, and mirrored, not directly and immediately experienced. Its obliquity is indicated from the first moment of his waking as the window sash, catching the light of the morning sun, casts a shadow upon the curtains. A sparrow slants across the sunlight and listens with

Quentin to the chimes striking the hour. A bird, or something flying, accompanies him in his recollections as well as in his walk. The hands of the clocks in the jeweler's window are "at a faint angle, like a gull tilting into the wind" (104). The gull image is associated with time (and death) by Quentin's father: "time is your misfortune Father said. A gull on an invisible wire attached through space dragged" (123). The gull becomes the symbol for eternity, the meeting of time and space, as he watches Gerald Bland rowing on the river.

Quentin notices mayflies slanting (136), girls gushing like "swallows swooping" (125), the river glinting "beyond things in sort of swooping glints" (130), and butterflies slanting along in the shade avoiding the slanting sunlight as they play about the boys going for a swim (141). As he tries to talk with the little Italian girl, "little sister," who follows him about silently, he hears "a bird somewhere in the woods, beyond the broken and infrequent slanting of sunlight" whose whistle to him is "a sound meaningless and profound" (154) because he recollects another time—after his empty and hopeless formal gesture of hitting Ames (while standing on the bridge over the water symbolizing Caddy's sexual sin and his own death impulse)—when "the sun slanted and a bird [was] singing somewhere beyond the sun" (179).

At that time, too, Ames appeared as if Quentin were "looking at him through a piece of coloured glass" (180), and as Quentin sought the shade of a tree, still stunned from fainting (Ames had not hit him), he "heard the bird again and the water and then everything sort of rolled away and I didnt feel anything at all I felt almost good after all those days and the nights with honeysuckle coming up out of the darkness into my room where I was trying to sleep" (180-81). And finally, Caddy's eyes, which were like cornered rats when Benjy smelled her sin with Dalton Ames (168), become empty "like the eyes in the statues blank and unseeing and serene" (182) as she repeats Ames's name and looks "off into the trees where the sun slanted and where the bird [sang]" (182). Immediately after this recollection Quentin feels his own eye "dead" and tries to see himself—by reflection—in the water in which Shreve is bathing it, since, as he learns, he has just had a fight with Bland.

The feel of obliquity is reinforced by Quentin's awareness of ascent and descent. Benjy reports that after Caddy had splashed Quentin with water in the branch scene, Quentin watched the others go up the hill toward the lights of the house (42). Years later, Quentin runs back down the hill toward the branch and out of

Benjy's bellowing where he finds Caddy lying half in the branch, "the water flowing about her hips" (168). Then, after a fumbling suicide attempt, with overtones of incest, they ascend the hill again (172) to meet Dalton Ames, where again, Caddy's and Ames's shadows merge in an image of obliquity to form one shadow with her head above his (173), and then the reverse, Ames's shadow high with Caddy's face becoming blurred (174), appearing to Quentin as *"the beast with two backs"* (167).

Quentin is particularly sensitive to shadow since he identifies his own coming death with shadow. He seems attracted to the Negro lore that "a drowned man's shadow was watching for him in the water all the time" (109), and several times feels he has "tricked" (109, 111, 114, 153) his shadow out of the water to follow him and allow him to tramp upon it (the shadow is an image of the body which he shall soon do away with): "trampling my shadow's bones into the concrete" (115), "walked upon the belly of my shadow" (115), "treading my shadow into pavement" (119), and "I stood in the belly of my shadow" (119). The "trick" is in accord with his whole personal attack upon reality, his refusal to recognize reality's inexorable warning when the shadow of the sash on the curtains put him "in time again, hearing the watch" (95). Even his own death as shadow is not, as his father recognizes, truly real to him: "you seem to regard it merely as an experience that will whiten your hair overnight so to speak without altering your appearance at all" (196). Shadow, shade, darkness, greyness, twilight are also somewhat equivalent to all sex. It was in the twilight that he first met Dalton Ames with Caddy, but his own virginity and self-identity are threatened by "so many of them walking along in the shadows and whispering with their soft girlvoices lingering in the shadowy places and the words coming out and perfume and eyes you could feel not see, but if it was that simple to do it wouldnt be anything *and if it wasnt anything, what was I"* (166, italics mine). Mrs. Bland, breaking into his reverie, appropriately diagnoses his case with the question, "Quentin? Is he sick, Mr MacKenzie?" (166).

The obliquity of external reality to Quentin is apparent in its slanted, shaded, half-hidden and mysterious character and also in its appearance as reflected and not directly present. To find himself after his fight with Bland, Quentin looks for his reflection in the water basin (182). He gazes over the side of a bridge spanning the Charles River, looking for his shadow, narcissistically seeking the profile of his death there, tricking it out of the water (it is, after all, a reflection of his body and not of his intellectual being) to refrain a while longer "from the waiting willing friendly tender incredible body of his beloved" (9). His entire last day is a court-ship of death; Julio's charge has symbolic substance; "You steala my seester" (158). Quentin's thievery (his namesake was also a thief) was of Caddy's innocence and now it is of his own life. Caddy found death *for him* at French Lick. His recollection of Caddy's marriage (only thirty-eight days before the time of his narration) is mirrored, shadowed, substanceless, and dominated by Benjy's bellowing:

> *Only she was running already when I heard it* [Benjy's bellowing]. *In the mirror she was running before I knew what it was. That quick, her train caught up over her arm she ran out of the mirror like a cloud, her veil swirling in long glints her heels brittle and fast clutching her dress onto her shoulder with the other hand, running out of the mirror the smells roses roses the voice that breathed o'er Eden. Then she was across the porch I couldn't hear her heels then in the moonlight like a cloud, the floating shadow of the veil running across the grass, into the bellowing.* (100-01)

In the last paragraph of his section, Quentin symbolically measures external reality again in the mirror. He looks for the bloodstain on his vest: "in the mirror the stain didnt show. Not like my eye did, anyway" (197).

The images of obliquity, then, pile up, come pell-mell—slanting, shadow, reflection—as Quentin reports and recalls. His final con-dition shows him to have fixed his life in images which allow reality to present experience only in their terms. The images re-veal his final condition as one in which he despairs of sustaining the meaning he has demanded of life; they show him estranged from any reference wider than his private problem, symbolically forcing the question of ultimate meaning, and finding experience to yield only emptiness. Faulkner affords Quentin a sentence near the end of his section which summarizes, in some of the familiar symbolic images, the three stages of his problem. Through his mind runs the question, when will the smell of wistaria stop?

> Sometimes I could put myself to sleep saying that over and over until after the honeysuckle got all mixed up in it the whole thing came to symbolise night and unrest I seemed to be lying neither asleep nor awake looking down a long corridor of grey halflight where *all stable things had become shadowy paradoxical* all I had

done shadows all I had felt suffered taking visible form antic and
perverse mocking without relevance inherent themselves with the
denial of the significance they should have affirmed thinking *I was
I was not who was not was not who.* (188, italics mine)

In this passage, the smell of wistaria is associated with his mother's
sickness, her incapacity to function as a mother. This odor yields
to honeysuckle as he fixes upon Caddy as the sex object embodying
his problem of meaning. Then night, unrest, a long corridor of
grey half-light, and shadow dominate his consciousness as his problem is stated in the abstract terms of time and being.

Immediately following this reverie Quentin reports that he
"could smell the curves of the river beyond the dusk" and could
see "the last light supine and tranquil upon tideflats like pieces
of broken mirror" (188). Reality is fractured in Quentin's broken
mirror, but in "the river beyond the dusk" he will seek in drowning
his "refuge unfailing[,] in which conflict [is] tempered[,] silenced
[and] reconciled" (188-89). He sees his suicide as a seeking of silence.
Moving from sex through time to pose the problem of being itself,
he despairs of saving meaning. He seeks the silence of non-being
in the swift and peaceful water of the river, where he can, as he
could not with Caddy, isolate himself "out of the loud world" and
let the world "roar away" (195)—its ticking watches, clanging
chimes, and the bellowing and moaning of Benjy. His father ex-
presses for him the object of this last desperate strategy: "you are
contemplating an apotheosis in which a temporary state of mind
will become symmetrical above the flesh and aware both of itself
and of the flesh it will not quite discard you will not even be dead"
(195-96). Quentin affirms his father's statement by the single word
"temporary." His father then touches the heart of the matter: "you
cannot bear to think that someday it will no longer hurt you like
this" (196).

Quentin's suicide, then, arises from despair at the prospect of
time's dulling even the meager meaning he has salvaged—his own
hurt. He is anxious about ultimate meaninglessness and emptiness
in time. His is a peculiarly modern as opposed to a Stoic or Christian anxiety. . . .

Although the dominant theme remains the same in Jason's section, an abrupt shift occurs in both the character of the narrator
and the narrative technique. Together these two accomplish a shift
of emphasis within the theme from the loss of meaning to the complete absence of meaning. . . .

As Jason runs through the events of his day . . . two images of him emerge. The first, his self-image, is of one victimized by life, yet able, by virtue of his own righteous strength and consummate rational power, to survive in a world from which he can force the satisfactions of his own rectitude. . . . His self-image is not just a straw man; obviously the very condition of his life is outrageous. In terms of his own inner logic, he has indeed been dealt with poorly, and his survival in the face of his inherited circumstance shows a certain neurotic vitality. His father *was* an alcoholic, his older brother a suicide; his sister *is* a prostitute, his brother an idiot, his niece a bitch, his uncle a toady and a drunkard. He *is* a victim of the stock market. Even from without his point of view, many of the conditions of his life are unjust. . . .

But the second image of Jason, the reader's, . . . is of a man who successfully distorts reality to provide it with a meaning commensurate with his own demands. . . . He appropriates the rational character of the Stoic attitude at those points where he can turn it to use, but he greatly attenuates its humanistic spirit to apply it only to himself. . . . Like the mythical Jason of Euripides, boasting to Medea of his magnanimity in bringing her from barbaric Colchis to civilized Greece, incapable of gratitude and thinking of his ambition only, Jason Compson measures justice exclusively in terms of self-advantage. . . . There is in his sane world no question of guilt or innocence in a Christian sense, but only of criminal defection from the attenuated norm, a norm established with reference to his cash advantage. . . . To say that Jason is "the first sane Compson since before Culloden" is to point up that Jason is not really a Compson at all. . . .

Faulkner has said of Jason that he represents "complete evil." Yet . . . he is more complex than that. Indeed, in many ways Jason is the most complex character in the novel, and the most difficult to assess. . . . For as Jason desperately accentuates his vanities to the point of pure evil, he appears in many respects innately incapable of any other response. If for the moment we can think of Dilsey as exemplifying the appropriate and saving response to the situation of the Compsons in 1928, we see in contrast that Jason seems temperamentally, psychologically, and even biologically so constituted that he *cannot* respond with love or forgiveness or even a natural human kindness to others. To the extent that there is this note of skeptical despair in Faulkner, it roots in the Stoic side of his estimate of man. Fate has dealt unevenly with men. Not all men in the Stoic scheme are capable of the response of the wise man; indeed, the mass of men are blatantly common. Jason

simply does not as a human being have what it takes. To this extent, his character exhibits a natural evil, not a distinctly human
one, which in turn causes real suffering. In the fact that Faulkner
does not in the novel's final issue allow this note to emerge as
purely skeptical, we can see something of a Calvinistic judgment
on his part upon the predamned. . . .

The second major theme of *The Sound and the Fury*, the positive status of meaning in experience, is achieved by refractions of
the . . . main actions through the characters of Benjy and Dilsey.
. . . Both Benjy and Dilsey stand in something of a choric relationship to the . . . main actions, reflecting, responding to, interpreting (dramatically, not intellectually) the events of the novel.
Dilsey, however, also involves herself directly in the action. . . .

When caution has been taken to keep Benjy's idiocy from being
lost from view, certain aesthetic and thematic facts remain to establish him as a carrier of the novel's positive theme. That he functions mainly as a contrast to Quentin is seen not only by the fact
that both are concerned primarily with the same period, but also
by the fact that in many ways they seem to share the same reality,
even responding often in apparently the same way to that reality.

Images of obliquity—shadow, reflection, slanting, ascent and
descent—fill Benjy's section too. Like Quentin, he sees his shadow
walk as he walks (65) and even notices that his shadow is higher on
the fence than Luster's (24). He marks "a bird slanting and tilting"
(24) and "the sun slanting on the broad grass" (70), sees *"slanting
holes"* in the barn roof *"full of spinning yellow"* (32) (Quentin
sees the "spinning sky" [134] reflected in the water), notes ascent
and descent as he goes to the Patterson's with Caddy or walks from
the branch to the house, and records the sensations of drunkenness
in terms of obliquity. Mirrors are prominent in his section also.
Jason and Caddy fight in the mirror (83); there are two fires, one
in his mother's room and one in the mirror (80); as his angle of
vision changes, fires appear and disappear in mirrors. In the
library there is "the dark tall place on the wall" where the mirror
once stood, and Benjy says "it was like a door, only it wasn't a
door" (79-80).

Many of the images are the same, yet the reality they imply is
only superficially coincident with Quentin's; the images occur to
Quentin and Benjy with a fundamentally different feel. The images
of obliquity are for Quentin the entire content of his experience;
they indicate the limits of his interpretation of reality in that final

stage where being itself becomes his private problem. Only by an overinterpretation of reality, the product of a precious intellectualization where an object is less real than its shadow, where events reflected and reflected upon are more actual than they are in their full immediacy, is Quentin able to maintain a coherent experience at all. . . .

. . . Benjy's inability to reason, to see implications, to regard events in total context, means that in the last analysis his effectiveness as a carrier of the positive theme is quite limited in a rational sense, and his self-centered idiocy effectively undercuts any tendency the reader might have to exalt his nonrationality.

Symbolically, however, there is wisdom in Benjy's senses; he clearly points the way, indicates the direction, embodies the fundamental elements of the solution to the problems posed by the negative theme. For example, unlike Quentin, he associates Caddy with the life-suggesting trees, not with the sex- and death-suggesting water. Water cleanses Caddy (of perfume, of Charlie's taint) for Benjy. He loves Caddy and firelight, while Quentin associates fire with a private hell in which he and Caddy expiate a sin they cannot commit. Benjy too has a demand for order, and if it is limited, it is at least an order present and meaningful, not lost and devitalized. His birthday does not fall on the day of resurrection and hope, but neither does it fall on the day of crucifixion and despair. These are slight evidences upon which to pin the presence of an affirmative theme, but they are nonetheless there as symbolic contrasts. Mere love, sheer revulsion from evil, is not enough, but it is a place from which to start. Like Jason, Benjy simply "does not have it" in fact, but unlike Jason, he does have it in principle.

It is in the character of Dilsey that the greatest evidence for a fulfilling meaning in experience lies . . . . More than any other character, Dilsey exemplifies a realistic living in the face of the event's full force. . . . In her character we are pushed beyond the rational, not to deny it, but to affirm that it is neither all of life nor enough of life. . . .

Dilsey's vision of the first and the last can be interpreted in a variety of ways—the Alpha and Omega of the Christ event she has just experienced in church, the beginning of the Compson misery in Mr. Compson and its end in Jason, the first of the various Compson children (she reared them all) and their final pathetic states, the first and the last in the metaphorical sense that all chronological events are in the hands of God whose sacrifice she has just rehearsed, or, in terms of their exemplification of human virtues, the paradoxical reversal of the first who shall be last (Jason) and the last who shall be first (Benjy). . . .

. . . [Dilsey gives] endlessly of herself to counter the very events which undo the Compsons. . . . Dilsey experiences it all, from the beginning to the end, and endures. Neither a philosopher nor a fool, she not only fights the battle but wins it. She, with Benjy, stands as a contradiction, a denial that the responses of the Compsons are inevitable and unavoidable. Her judgment upon them is in her whole character, her whole life, for they could have made the same response to the events which she made, a response of love, self-sacrifice, compassion, and pity.

The response of love is not only her greatest comment upon the Compsons, but it is also her way of actively engaging the evil of their situation. For Dilsey does, as the others do not, attack the basic situation with the tools at hand. Benjy responds in principle in the same way as Dilsey, but is atrophied in fact by the limitations of his psyche. In Dilsey we have the fully developed response of the compassionate human being and the most effective carrier of the affirmative theme. Her singing, "repetitive, mournful and plaintive, austere" (286), is symbolic of the realistic courage which allows her, in the face of the most devastating evidences of meaninglessness, to find "de power en de glory" (313).

Unresolved Tensions

by *Walter J. Slatoff*

. . . Many . . . aspects of [Faulkner's] presentation . . . resist rational analysis and leave us with an unresolved suspension of varied or opposed suggestions. A large number of Faulkner's extended metaphors, for example, have these qualities. This partial description of the sermon of the visiting preacher in *The Sound and the Fury* is characteristic.

> He tramped steadily back and forth . . . hunched, his hands clasped behind him. He was like a worn small rock whelmed by the successive waves of his voice. With his body he seemed to feed the voice that, succubus like, had fleshed its teeth in him. And the congregation seemed to watch with its own eyes while the voice consumed him, until he was nothing and they were nothing and there was not even a voice but instead their hearts were speaking to one another in chanting measures beyond the need for words, so that when he came to rest against the reading desk, his monkey face lifted and his whole attitude that of a serene, tortured crucifix that transcended its shabbiness and insignificance and made it of no moment, a long moaning expulsion of breath rose from them, and a woman's single soprano: "Yes, Jesus!" (p. 310)

In context the passage has considerable emotional force and conveys a sense of the minister's power and effect on the congregation. On the other hand, it is full of opposed and varied suggestions which resist rational integration. We shift from naturalistic description to a simile in which the preacher is likened to a rock and his voice to waves. The voice then acquires teeth, and "succubus like" (i.e., like an *evil* spirit!) consumes him. Is the ugliness of the

"Unresolved Tensions," [Editor's title,] by Walter J. Slatoff. From "The Edge of Order: The Pattern of Faulkner's Rhetoric," Twentieth Century Literature, *III (October, 1957), 107-27. This article is also to be found in* Quest for Failure: A Study of William Faulkner *(Ithaca: Cornell University Press, 1960), pp. 137-39, 155-58. Copyright © 1960 by Cornell University. Condensed and reprinted with the permission of the publisher.*

image intentional, we wonder. Does Faulkner perhaps add teeth because they are in antithesis to the "suck" suggestion of "succubus"? The minister and the congregation become "nothing" but still have hearts. There is no voice, but the hearts "speak" to one another, although without words. We are then reminded of the naturalistic monkey face immediately before the preacher's body (which was a "rock," fleshly food, "nothing," and a speaking "heart") becomes suggestive of a crucifix, at once "serene" and "tortured," "that transcended its [the attitude's? the crucifix's?] shabbiness and insignificance." Upon close examination even the general nature of the experience of the congregation is perplexing, because there is the implication of a peaceful speaking of hearts and then of release of tension. Faulkner's mixed metaphors of this sort are not occasional accidents, for in general he makes no effort to keep them consistent and often makes use of the most "mixed" for his most important communications. And as in the oxymoron, the irresolvable elements are not accidental but seem an integral part of structure. . . .

Probably the most crucial indication of Faulkner's intentions is the fact that the endings of all his novels not only fail to resolve many of the tensions and meanings provided in the novels but also seem carefully designed to prevent such resolution. Above all, they leave unresolved the question of the meaningfulness of the human efforts and suffering we have witnessed, whether the sound and the fury is part of some larger design or whether it has signified nothing in an essentially meaningless universe.

Consider, for example, the final section of *The Sound and the Fury*, which is perhaps Faulkner's most unified and tightly woven novel. . . . The final section of the book, narrated from an omniscient and objective point of view, begins with a focus and emphasis that seem to offer a kind of implicit interpretation and resolution, one in accord with the sentiments and mood of Faulkner's Nobel Prize speech. The strong emphasis on Dilsey's fortitude, decency, and Christian humility and on her comprehensive view of time . . . provides a context for the unhappy events, a perspective from which to view them and a way to feel about them. On the other hand, this episode does not so much offer a synthesis or interpretation as a general vantage point and degree of moral affirmation. It does not help us to understand most of the particulars of the Compson story any better, to illuminate, say, the character and motives of Quentin and Caddy. Nor does it in any but a peripheral way relate to the socioeconomic context of the story.

Although it asserts the relevance of Christianity to the story it does not really clarify the nature of that relevance nor make clear how seriously we are to take the Christian context. . . .

. . . The emphasis on Dilsey and her trip to church is at the beginning of the final section and is only one of several emphases in that section. It is followed by the lengthy description of Jason's vain and tormenting pursuit of Quentin, which provides a very different perspective, mood, and set of feelings. We are back in a realm of sound and fury, even of melodrama. We do not see Jason from the large perspective we have just shared with Dilsey, but respond to his frustration and defeat with a grim amusement and satisfaction only slightly leavened by pity. . . . It is true that we might draw a sharp contrast between the ways Dilsey and Jason spend their Sunday and between Dilsey's sense of Christian acceptance and Jason's violent and impatient paranoia, and we might go on to contrast her slow and decorous walk to church with his frenzied dependence on the automobile, and these contrasts can be related to the general contrast between traditional and traditionless cultures. Here again, however, one cannot quite understand the relevance of the contrast except as generalized ironic commentary. Nor do we, I think, actually feel this contrast while reading this section. Essentially Dilsey and her church have receded into the landscape and seem barely relevant to Jason's predicament.

The final part of the last section emphasizes Benjy's misery and the callousness and swagger of Dilsey's grandson, Luster, as he torments Benjy, first by taking his bottle, then by shouting "Caddy," and finally by driving around the square in the wrong direction. We are reminded for a moment of Dilsey's decency and faith but only to feel its ineffectualness, for neither she nor the church service has touched Luster. The book closes with the carriage ride of Luster and Benjy. . . . It is a powerful ending and a fitting one in its focus on Benjy and its application to the general theme of order and disorder running through the novel. But it is an ending which provides anything but a synthesis or resolution, and it leaves us with numerous conflicting feelings and ideas. We are momentarily relieved and pleased by the cessation of Benjy's suffering, but we are troubled by the fact that it has been achieved by Jason, who cares nothing for Benjy and is concerned only with maintaining an external and superficial decorum. We can hardly draw any real satisfaction from the serenity and order, because the serenity is the "empty" serenity of an idiot and the order is that demanded by an idiot. The general tenor of the episode is in accord with Mr. Compson's pessimism rather than Faulkner's Nobel Prize speech, for everything in it suggests the meaninglessness and futility of life.

This final scene does not negate the moderate affirmation of the Dilsey episode, nor does it really qualify it. Rather it stands in suspension with it as a commentary of equal force. We feel and are intended to feel, I think, that the events we have witnessed are at once tragic and futile, significant and meaningless. We cannot move beyond this.

"Form, Solidity, Color"

by Hyatt H. Waggoner

In the year in which *The Sound and the Fury* was published Faulkner made a point, for a while, of carrying a cane and wearing spats, serving notice on Oxfordians of the role he had chosen for himself. The young artist had not yet been acknowledged as artist. There would be time later for him to adopt the role of Mississippi farmer.

But the mask of the artist was not merely a gesture of defiance of local mores. . . . The spats and the cane were the young artist's substitute for the beret he had worn briefly in Paris. *The Sound and the Fury* was created in the context in which Joyce, Pound, Eliot, Gertrude Stein, Conrad, the later James, and Ford Madox Ford were finding ways of expressing a new sensibility. . . . *The Sound and the Fury* is the first book in which Faulkner was able consistently to practice his art as he had come to conceive it. . . . The result is a "passion week of the heart" that makes clear how sensitive and creative was Faulkner's response to the new symbolic techniques of such writers as Joyce and Eliot. *The Sound and the Fury* is very much a product of the twenties, by which of course I do not mean that it is "dated" in a bad sense. . . .

In one sense, [however,] *The Sound and the Fury* continues in modified form the tradition of nineteenth-century fiction. It tells the story of a family over a period of about thirty years, following a generation from early childhood through the chief remembered events of their lives to maturity or death. . . . Though the manner of telling is untraditional . . . , the story told is more like the

"Form, Solidity, Color." From William Faulkner: From Jefferson to the World, by Hyatt H. Waggoner. (*Lexington: University of Kentucky Press, 1959*), Chap. 3. Copyright © *1959 by the University of Kentucky Press. Condensed and reprinted with the permission of the publisher. In the original essay, Waggoner discusses more fully the "traditional" aspects of the novel and the technical problems its order of presentation presents. He also offers fuller and sensible analyses of Benjy, Quentin, Jason, and Dilsey.*

story told in *David Copperfield* or *Henry Esmond* than like that told in *Ulysses*. Here it is not the shifting of a cake of soap from one pocket to another that reminds us of the outer, objective world but death, marriage, and death again. In *Ulysses* the events of Bloom's day, as they are in themselves, are most trivial. The significance lies chiefly in what they are made to recall by being placed in a framework of echo and allusion. In *The Sound and the Fury* the events themselves are significant: recast in a different telling, they would serve for a traditional, pre-Joycean novel. That they are *not* told in that manner is of course of the essence; but we should not lose sight of what is told in our concentration on the manner of telling. . . .

. . . It is true that if we center our attention not on the larger aspects of structure, on the arrangement of the sections and the relation of this arrangement to the story being told, but on the smaller units of structure, on the order of events within any one of the first three sections, we may get the impression of disorder. But this "disorder" is of a kind to which we are thoroughly accustomed by now, the shuffling back and forth in memory between past and present; and there is a significant, a very immediate and human point of view from which it seems not "disorder" at all but *our* kind of order, the order of human experience, human reality, before "inward" and "outward" are abstracted from the whole, separated. If this mixing up of events from past and present puts a barrier in the way of the inexperienced or inattentive reader, it contributes to the illusion of reality felt by the prepared reader. . . . The blending of past and present in the novel may make some passages difficult at first reading, but the final effect is to focus and clarify both past and present. . . .

The novel may be said to move from the concrete to the abstract, in several senses. It moves from Benjy, immersed in time and able to hold its treasures only because he is unable to think in abstractions; to Quentin, who mediates on time and longs for assurance that values are timeless, but who can escape from time only into death; to Jason, who is concerned with the concrete moment only insofar as it can be translated into his "practical realities," money and power, which are finally as abstract as Quentin's "honor"; to Dilsey, whose faith in timeless intangibles enables her to live in time and deal with concrete experience without frustration and without despair. . . .

In still another sense the novel moves from the concrete to the abstract: it moves, in the successive sections, from the sensory to the interpretive, from Benjy through Quentin and Jason to Dilsey. The arrangement is essentially one we might call "inductive" if the word did not suggest logic rather than art. The structure of the novel, in short, invites us to participate in the process by which the judgments implicit in the last section are arrived at, invites us by first immersing us in the facts and then arranging for us a series of perspectives. Quentin's and Jason's perspectives are opposite in character and quality but alike in subjecting the raw data of Benjy's perception to Procrustean interpretations, "idealistic" or "realistic." The last section moves beyond realism and idealism, affirming at once the qualitative richness of Benjy's experience and the human values which he was partially able to respond to but unable to define or protect, implicitly acknowledging the values Quentin was unable effectively to believe in and Jason cynically denied.

The "objectivity" of the last section is, then, only formal: the reporting seems objective because we have known Benjy, Quentin, and Jason. We have been immersed in experience, and in two versions of experience-as-interpreted: when we stand off and look at what we have known, it looks the way we see it in the last section. The objectivity here is a technical achievement made possible by the total form of the work; its implicit perspective is based on judgments which we ourselves have been brought to the point of making. If the last section is in one sense the simplest, in another it is the most complex.

Structurally, then, and at the deepest level of meaning, there are movements in two directions going on here. Benjy's experience is at once more subjective and more trustworthy than Jason's. Quentin's view of life, and the resultant shape of his experience, are at once more "realistic"—because not dependent on an act of faith —and more subjective than Dilsey's. Paradox is at the center of the vision. The order achieved in the last section has been achieved through difficulty, formally and thematically. The easy-reading, formalized, traditional order of the last section would be, aesthetically, too easy if the three sections that precede it had not prepared us for the narrator's way of ordering, just as, religiously, Dilsey's affirmation of a supersensible order would be too easy if she had never suffered the sound and the fury. Insofar as we can achieve an unbiased reading of the novel, our faith in Dilsey is a response both to the order which we have seen her bring to the lives she touches and to the order which her section brings to the book.

Theme and structure are one thing in *The Sound and the Fury*. Both assert the possibility of achieving a difficult order out of the chaotic flux of time.

The possibility; a difficult order. There is little joy in this Easter day. Dilsey wears purple, a liturgical color that suggests the sadness of penitential seasons—the color for Advent and Lent. It is not without its meaning that the saving positive values, the ordering beliefs, are embodied here in an idiot and in a representative of an ignorant and despised people. As the words that might save us come to us fragmented and in an unknown tongue at the end of *The Waste Land,* so the Word here is revealed only in the senseless bawling of an idiot and proclaimed only by the bells ringing down in "Nigger Hollow." The novel allows us to make of this what we will, and we shall make somewhat different interpretations of it depending on our fundamental beliefs. But there are perhaps a few aspects of the theme on which we may all agree.

Our first reaction as we try to hold the whole work in mind and think of its meaning for us may well be a sense of the impossibility of thus wrenching apart "form" and "content," even temporarily and after preparation. The reaction may well be a sound one, and at any rate constitutes an implicit tribute to the richness, solidity, the full aesthetic achievement of this work. But we can and do, sometimes usefully, generalize about the meanings embodied in works of art; it is not impossible to do so here. First, then, we note that by the end of the novel there has been a reversal of the meaning first suggested by the title, or at least a significant qualification of it. The idiot has turned out to be the carrier of the values we accept: the tale he tells signifies much, and if one of its meanings is that life is at last "a stalemate of dust and desire," it is only one, and not the one that the idiot himself suggests to us. Nor Dilsey. In her innocent ignorance she continues to live by what was once, according to St. Paul, "foolishness to the Greeks" and is still foolishness to Jason.

But the sound and the fury will not be dismissed as unreal, or the private fate and preoccupation of the Compsons. If the saving values are no longer held except by an idiot and an ignorant old woman—and, in a sense, putatively, by a maladjusted neurotic heading for suicide—then they are effectively lost to us. Quentin cannot simply *decide* to believe in the reality of sin, and so in the reality of a timeless order. In this fictional counterpart of *The Waste Land* a situation is presented and diagnosed: no remedy is proposed. The flower Benjy clutches as the shapes flow by in the final scene has a broken stem, and Jason has effectively prevented him from reaching the cemetery. When they turn to the left around the square Benjy can only bawl his grief, not re-establish the right direction. The fact that he bawls is the final reminder to us of his role as a Christ image: in folklore, the *left* has often been associated with the *sinister*, as the etymology of *sinister* itself reminds us. But the fact that he can do nothing more than bawl is also a final reminder that this Christ is powerless; the Word swaddled in darkness, "unable to speak a word."

Only when we import into our consideration of this novel ideas we have gained from other, later Faulkner stories are we likely to feel that we can confidently resolve this ambiguity. If we think of the role played by the Negro in the later fiction, in which he sometimes achieves an explicitly redemptive status by endurance and acceptance of suffering, we may be tempted to resolve completely the irony of Dilsey's Easter; too completely, I think, as though we were to read all the meaning of the *Four Quartets* back into *The Waste Land* because we have discovered its potentiality there.

Yet we may say that from the apparent meaninglessness of Compson history, something has emerged, some meaning, some value, some real if not publicly recognized order. If instead we say that out of the obscure and fragmentary expressions of inward experience that form the first three sections, Dilsey and Ben and Mother and Jason emerge as characters in the final, objective section and a story emerges there whole and clear and ready for our judgment, we shall be saying very much the same thing. Every aspect of the form is functional here—but to say even that is to imply a dichotomy that does not exist. As the plot is "hidden," so the theme is hidden. As characters finally emerge, full-bodied and wholly memorable, from a texture and structure that may seem until we have completed our reading too lyric and fragmented to produce character, so a dramatic impact unexcelled in the modern novel remains as a final impression of a novel in no obvious or traditional sense dramatic.

One way of putting the greatness of *The Sound and the Fury* is to say that we begin by seeing it as a marvelously precise and solid evocation of a specific time and place and family and end by realizing that it is more than this, that the concrete has become universal: an anatomy of a world, a world recreated, analyzed, and judged as it can be in only the greatest fiction.

Appendix: Chronology and Scene Shifts in Benjy's and Quentin's Sections

by Edmond L. Volpe

Section I—Chronology of Scenes

No dates are given for those scenes which, from the evidence in the novel, cannot be assigned to a specific year. They are, however, set in their chronological order. The double date assigned to two scenes indicates that the year was established according to Caddy's age. Without knowing the month of her birth, we cannot be certain which of the dates is correct.

"Chronology and Scene Shifts in Benjy's and Quentin's Sections." [Editor's title.] From A Reader's Guide to William Faulkner, *by Edmond L. Volpe. (New York: Farrar, Straus & Giroux, 1964), pp. 353, 363-65, 373-77. Copyright © 1964 by Edmond L. Volpe. Reprinted and adapted by permission of the publisher. Page numbers in the first column of each "Guide to the Scene Shifts" refer to the most recent Modern Library and 1929 editions of the novel. For a slightly more detailed ordering of the scenes in Benjy's section, see George R. Stewart and Joseph M. Backus, "'Each in Its Ordered Place': Structure and Narrative in 'Benjy's Section' of* The Sound and the Fury," *American Literature, XXIX (January, 1958), 440-56.*

Scene	Date	Benjy's Attendant
Damuddy's Death	1898	Versh
Benjy's Name Changed	1900 (Nov.)	
Dec. 23: Delivery of Message		
End of Uncle Maury-Patterson Affair		
Caddy Uses Perfume	1905-6	T.P.
Caddy in the Swing	1906-7	
Benjy, 13, Must Sleep Alone	1908	
Caddy's Loss of Virginity	1909 (Late Summer)	
Caddy's Wedding	1910 (April 24)	
Benjy at the Gate	1910 (May)	
Quentin's Suicide	1910 (June 2)	
Benjy Attacks the Burgess Girl and Is Castrated		
Death of Mr. Compson	1912	
Trip to Cemetery		
Death of Roskus		Luster
The Present	1928 (April 7)	

Section I—Guide to the Scene Shifts

First Words of Scene			
1	Through the fence	Present	
3	*Caddy uncaught me*	Dec. 23	
3	It's too cold	Dec. 23	
5	*What are you*	Present	
5	What is it.	Dec. 23	
8	*Cant you shut up*	Present	
9	Git in, now,	Trip to Cemetery	
13	Cry baby,	Present	
13	Keep your hands	Dec. 23	
14	*Mr Patterson*	End of P. Affair	
15	They aint nothing	Present	
19	*and Roskus came*	Damuddy's Death	
22	*What is the matter*	Present	
22	Roskus came	Damuddy's Death	
23	*See you all*	Present	
23	If we go slow,	Damuddy's Death	
23	*The cows came*	Caddy's Wedding	
26	*At the top*	Damuddy's Death	
33	*There was a fire*	Quentin's Death	
34	*Taint no luck*	Quentin's Death	
35	*Take him and*	Death of Mr. C.	
38	*You cant go yet*	Mr. C.'s Funeral	
38	*Come on,*	Present	
38	Frony and T. P.	Damuddy's Death	
39	*They moaned*	Death of Roskus	
39	"Oh." Caddy said	Damuddy's Death	
39	*Dilsey moaned,*	Death of Roskus	
40	I like to know	Damuddy's Death	
40	The bones rounded	Death of Mr. C.	
42	*I had it*	Present	
42	Do you think	Damuddy's Death	
44	*When we looked*	Caddy's Wedding	
45	A snake crawled	Damuddy's Death	
45	*You aint got*	Caddy's Wedding	
45	We stopped	Damuddy's Death	
45	*They getting*	Caddy's Wedding	
46	They haven't	Damuddy's Death	
47	*I saw them.*	Caddy's Wedding	
48	*Benjy, Caddy said,*	C. Uses Perfume	
51	Come on, now.	Benjy, 13	
52	Uncle Maury was	End of P. Affair	
53	You a big boy.	Benjy, 13	
54	*Caddy smelled*	Damuddy's Death	
55	*Where you want*	Present	
56	The kitchen was	Caddy in Swing	
56	*Luster came*	Present	
56	It was dark	Caddy in Swing	
56	*Come away*	Present	
56	It was two	Caddy in Swing	

58	*I kept a telling*	Present	
62	You cant do	Benjy at Gate	
63	*How did he*	B. Attacks Girl	
63	It was open	B. Attacks Girl	
64	and the bright	Castration	
64	*Here, loony,*	Present	
68	*What you want*	Name Change	
68	Aint you shamed	Present	
69	*I could hear*	Name Change	
70	I ate some	Present	
71	*That's right,*	Name Change	
71	The long wire	Present	
74	*Your name is*	Name Change	
75	Caddy said, "Let	Damuddy's Death	
75	*Versh set me*	Name Change	
76	*Mother's sick,*	Damuddy's Death	
76	*We could hear*	Name Change	
80	*Jason came in.*	Present	
80	You can look	Name Change	
81	Dilsey said,	Present	
81	*We could hear*	Name Change	
81	Quentin said,	Present	
82	*I could hear*	Name Change	
83	Dilsey said,	Present	
84	Versh smelled	Name Change	
84	We could hear	Loss Virginity	
84	Versh said,	Name Change	
85	We were in	Loss Virginity	
85	*What are you*	Present	
85	Versh said,	Name Change	
86	*Has he got*	Present	
86	Steam came off	Name Change	
86	*Now, now,*	Present	
86	It got down	Name Change	
87	*Yes he will,*	Present	
87	Roskus said,	Name Change	
87	*You've been*	Present	
87	Then I dont	Name Change	
87	*Oh, I wouldn't*	Present	
87	She sulling	Name Change	
87	*Quentin pushed*	Present	
87	Mother's sick	Name Change	
88	Goddamn you	Present	
88	Caddy gave me	Name Change	
88	*She smelled*	Present	
89	We didn't go	Damuddy's Death	
90	*Quentin,*	Present	
90	Quentin and	Damuddy's Death	
90	*I got undressed*	Present	
91	There were two	Damuddy's Death	

Section II—Chronology of Scenes

Scene	Date
Damuddy's Death and Benjy's Name Changed	1898, 1900
Natalie Scene	— —
Caddy Kisses a Boy	1906-7
Caddy's Loss of Virginity*	1909 (Late Summer)
The Wedding Announcement	1910
Quentin Meets Herbert	1910 (April 22)
The Eve of the Wedding	1910 (April 23)
The Wedding	1910 (April 24)
The Present (Quentin's Suicide)	1910 (June 2)

SECTION II—GUIDE TO THE SCENE SHIFTS

Quentin's thought association is rapid, and many of his memories are fused. I have attempted in the following listing to identify references to major scenes, such as "She ran right out of the mirror," a reference to Caddy's Wedding. Many of Quentin's thoughts, however, are not associated with remembered scenes. These thoughts, such as "Jason furnished the flour," are identified as thoughts about someone or something.

93	When the shadow	Present	106	But I thought	Christmas, 1909
95	*She ran right out*	Caddy's Wedding	108	I wouldn't begin	Grammar School
95	*Mr and Mrs Jason*	Announcement	109	*Moving sitting*	Natalie Scene
95	I said I have	Loss Virginity	109	*One minute she*	Loss Virginity
95	Shreve stood	Present	109	*I'm going to run*	Damuddy's Death
96	Calling Shreve	Quarrel, Spoade	109	*Dilsey.* ¶ *He*	Name Change
96	Because it means	Loss Virginity	108	The street car	Present
96	and Shreve said	Quarrel, Spoade	111	Benjy knew it	Damuddy's Death
96	Did you ever	Loss Virginity	111	The tug came	Present
96	Spoad was in	Present	113	*Did you ever*	Loss Virginity
97	*I have committed*	Loss Virginity	114	And after a while	Present
98	And I will look	Death by Drowning	114	*Harvard my*	Meets Herbert
98	Dalton Ames.	Loss Virginity	114	That pimple-faced	Caddy Kisses Boy
98	I went to the	Present	114	*He was lying*	Caddy's Wedding
100	*Only she was*	Caddy's Wedding	114	that could drive	Meets Herbert
100	Shreve said,	Present	115	Mr and Mrs Jason	Announcement

* The summer in which Caddy loses her virginity includes several important scenes: (1) After Caddy begins seeing Dalton Ames, Mr. Compson accuses Quentin of spying on her; Quentin denies doing so, Mr. Compson apologizes and talks to Quentin about Mrs. Compson and other matters; (2) Benjy smells Caddy's loss of virginity, Quentin confronts Caddy at the creek; (3) Quentin meets Dalton Ames on the bridge; (4) Mrs. Compson and Caddy leave for French Lick; (5) Quentin tries unsuccessfully to convince his father he has committed incest; they talk about suicide, the ravages of time, etc.

115	Country people	Meets Herbert	132	I saw you come	Meets Herbert
116	*Jason furnished the*	Jason as boy	137	*You're sick how*	Eve of Wedding
116	There was no	Present	137	Not that blackguard	Meets Herbert
116	Going to Harvard.	Pasture Sold	137	Now and then	Present
116	*He lay on the*	Caddy's Wedding	138	*That blackguard,*	Meets Herbert
116	*We have sold*	Pasture Sold	138	The river glinted	Present
116	You should have	Meets Herbert	138	*I'm sick you'll*	Eve of Wedding
117	*Father I have*	Loss Virginity	138	The car stopped	Present
117	Dont ask Quentin	Meets Herbert	138	*There was something*	Eve of Wedding
117	*My little sister*	Loss Virginity	139	I could still see	Present
117	Unless I do	Meets Herbert	139	*The street lamps*	Eve of Wedding
117	*A face reproachful*	Loss Virginity	139	*Then they told me*	Q. Breaks Leg
117	Hats not unbleached	Present	139	At last I couldn't	Present
118	I wouldn't have	Loss Virginity	140	*told me the bone*	Q. Breaks Leg
118	Trampling my	Present	140	Even sound seemed	Present
118	*I will not have*	Loss Virginity	141	Niggers. Louis	Hunting Trip
118	The chimes began	Present	142	*Got to marry*	Eve of Wedding
118	*think I would have*	Loss Virginity	143	I began to feel	Present
119	I walked upon	Present	142	*Caddy that*	Eve of Wedding
119	*feeling Father*	Loss Virginity	143	Versh told me	Castration Image
119	He was coming	Present	143	And Father said	Loss Virginity
124	*Lying on the*	Caddy's Wedding	143	Where the shadow	Present
124	He took one look	Loss Virginity	144	*If it could just*	Clean Flame Image
124	*The street lamps*	Loss Virginity	144	The arrow increased	Present
124	The chimes ceased	Present	149	Caddy that black-	
124	*go down the hill*	Loss Virginity		guard	Meets Herbert
124	Uncle Maury	Uncle M., Jason	149	Their voices came	Present
124	*Whyn't you keep*	D's Death—Jason	151	*Why must you*	Eve of Wedding
124	Rolling his head	Uncle M., Jason	151	Let's go up to	Present
124	Shreve was coming	Present	152	*Say it to Father*	Eve of Wedding
125	*The street lamps*	Loss Virginity	152	Ah, come on	Present
126	The car came up	Present	152	*it is because*	Loss Virginity
126	*your Mother's dream*	Pasture sold	152	He paid me no	Present
126	what have I done	Loss Virginity	152	*that blackguard*	Meets Herbert
128	If that was the	Present	153	Do you like fishing	Present
129	*Who would play*	Death Image	153	*Caddy that blackguard*	Eve of Wedding
129	Eating the business	Present	153	The boy turned	Present
130	*Dalton Ames*	Loss Virginity	153	*Else have I thought*	Eve of Wedding
130	*Quentin has shot*	Eve of Wedding	153	Some days in late	Present
130	background.	Present (Mrs. B.)	153	*But now I know*	Eve of Wedding
130	*always his voice*	Eve of Wedding	153	The buggy was	
130	an affinity for evil	Present (Mrs. B.)		drawn	Present
130	*Quentin has shot*	Eve of Wedding	154	*On what on your*	Eve of Wedding
130	tone of smug	Present (Mrs. B.)	154	His white shirt	Present
130	*the curtains*	Eve of Wedding	154	*Sold the pasture*	Eve of Wedding
130	*the voice that*	Caddy's Wedding	154	*one minute she was*	Loss Virginity
130	*clothes upon the*	Eve of Wedding	155	When you opened	Present
130	*by the nose seen*	Loss Virginity	159	*Seen the doctor*	Eve of Wedding
130	what he said?	Present (Mrs. B.)	159	Because women	Loss Virginity
131	*Are you going*	Eve of Wedding	160	You'd better take	Present
131	wondered who	Present (Mrs. B.)	160	*getting the odour*	Loss Virginity
132	*shot him through*	Eve of Wedding	160	We reached the	Present

166	getting honeysuckle	Loss Virginity
166	*What did you let*	Caddy Kisses Boy
166	The wall went	Present
166	*not a dirty girl*	Caddy Kisses Boy
167	*It was raining*	Natalie Scene
167	She walked just	Present
167	*I bet I can*	Natalie Scene
167	We went on	Present
168	*It's like dancing*	Natalie Scene
168	The road went on	Present
169	*I hold to use*	Natalie Scene
169	We began to hear	Present
169	*Stay mad.*	Natalie Scene
170	Hear them in	Present
170	*mud was warmer*	Natalie Scene
170	They saw us	Present
171	*We lay in the*	Natalie Scene
172	There's town	Present
172	*and the water*	Natalie Scene
172	Then we heard	Present
183	*ever do that*	Loss Virginity
183	They do, when	Present
183	*her knees her face*	Loss Virginity
183	Beer, too	Present
183	*like a thin wash*	Loss Virginity
183	You're not a	Present
183	*him between us*	Loss Virginity
184	No, I'm Canadian	Present
184	*talking about him*	Gerald and Ames
184	I adore Canada	Present
184	*with one hand*	Loss of Virginity
184	"No," Shreve said.	Present
184	*running the beast*	Sex image
184	*how many Caddy*	Eve of Wedding

184	Neither did I	Present
184	*I dont know*	Eve of Wedding
184	*Father I have*	Loss Virginity
184	and Gerald's	Present
184	*we did how can*	Loss Virginity
185	never be got to	Present
185	*did you love them*	Eve of Wedding
185	one minute she was	Loss Virginity
203	It kept on running	Present
213	*the first car*	Meets Herbert
213	*that's what Jason*	Jason
213	*Benjamin Benjamin*	Name Change
213	It took a lot	Present
214	*seeing on the*	Image: Ride Back to Bridge
214	I turned out	Present
214	*After they had*	Loss Virginity
215	When I was little	Boyhood Memory
215	Then the honey-suckle	Loss Virginity
215	*hands can see*	Boyhood Memory
215	My nose could see	Present
215	*yet the eyes*	Boyhood Memory
216	It was empty too	Present
216	*hands can see*	Boyhood Memory
216	I returned up	Present
216	*Aren't you ever*	Announcement
216	I am. Drink.	Present. Fused Thoughts
217	*as soon as she*	Loss Virginity
217	staying downstairs	Uncle M.'s Black Eye
219	The three quarters	Present
219	and that's it if	Caddy with Boys
219	and he we must	Loss Virginity
222	The last note	Present

Chronology of Important Dates

	Faulkner	Cultural and Historical Events
1890		Frazer, *The Golden Bough*; William James, *The Principles of Psychology*.
1894		Debussy, "Prelude à l'aprèsmidi d'un faune."
1897	Faulkner born, September 25, New Albany, Mississippi.	
1902	Moves to Oxford, Mississippi.	
1906		*The Education of Henry Adams.*
1913		Proust, *Du Côté de chez Swann;* Stravinsky, *Le Sacre du printemps.*
1917		United States enters World War I.
1918		Spengler, *The Decline of the West.*
1919	First published poem, "L'Apres-Midi d'un Faune."	Anderson, *Winesburg, Ohio.*
1920		Lewis, *Main Street*; English translation of Freud, *A General Introduction to Psychoanalysis.*
1922		Joyce, *Ulysses*; Eliot, *The Waste Land.*
1925	Travels in Europe, esp. Paris.	

1929	Marries Estelle Oldham; *Sartoris; The Sound and the Fury.*	Beginning of Great Depression.
1930	*As I Lay Dying.*	*I'll Take My Stand,* by "Twelve Southerners."
1931	*Sanctuary.*	
1932	*Light in August.*	Caldwell, *Tobacco Road.*
1935		Wolfe, *Of Time and the River.*
1936	*Absalom, Absalom!*	
1940	*The Hamlet.*	
1941		United States enters World War II.
1942	*Go Down, Moses.*	
1945		End of World War II.
1946	*The Portable Faulkner.*	Warren, *All the King's Men.*
1950	Awarded Nobel Prize.	
1951	Receives National Book Award for *Collected Stories.*	Salinger, *The Catcher in the Rye.*
1954	*A Fable.*	*Brown v. Board of Education of Topeka.*
1955	National Book Award and Pulitzer Prize.	
1962	*The Reivers.* Dies, June 6, Oxford.	

Notes on Editor and Contributors

MICHAEL H. COWAN, the editor of this volume, teaches at Yale University. He is the author of *City of the West: Emerson, America, and Urban Metaphor.*

EVELYN SCOTT, poet, novelist, memoirist, was best known for her Civil War novel, *The Wave,* published in the same year as *The Sound and the Fury.*

MAURICE COINDREAU taught for nearly forty years at Princeton before returning in 1961 to his native France. Author of *Aperçus de littérature americaine,* he has translated into French works by Faulkner, Hemingway, Caldwell, and Saroyan.

IRVING HOWE, prolific critic, teaches at Hunter College. Among his many works are *Politics and the Novel,* a collection of critical essays on Edith Wharton, and studies of Sherwood Anderson and Thomas Hardy.

OLGA VICKERY teaches at the Riverside branch of the University of California. She is co-editor of the influential collection, *William Faulkner: Three Decades of Criticism.*

PERRIN LOWREY formerly taught at the University of Chicago. He is the author of *The Great Speckled Bird and Other Stories.*

CLEANTH BROOKS, co-author of the highly influential *Understanding Poetry,* teaches at Yale. Among his many critical works are *Modern Poetry and the Tradition, The Well Wrought Urn,* and *The Hidden God.*

CARVEL COLLINS is now at Notre Dame, after many years on the faculty of M. I. T. He has edited much of Faulkner's early writing and is co-author of *Literature in the Modern World.*

LOUISE DAUNER teaches at the Indianapolis campus of the University of Indiana, where she is Assistant Chairman of the English Department.

ROBERT M. SLABEY is Associate Professor of English at the University of Notre Dame.

JOHN W. HUNT is Professor of English at Earlham College.

WALTER J. SLATOFF is Associate Professor of English at Cornell.

HYATT H. WAGGONER teaches at Brown. He is author of *The Heel of Elohim: Science and Values in Modern American Poetry* and *Hawthorne: A Critical Study*.

EDMOND L. VOLPE is Chairman of the Department of English at the City College of New York. He is co-editor of *Ten Modern Short Novels*.

Selected Bibliography

Readers should refer to the fuller original texts of many of the essays reprinted in this collection. In addition, the following may prove useful:

Backman, Melvin, *Faulkner: The Major Years.* Bloomington: Indiana University Press, 1966, pp. 13-40. General study, with stress on Quentin.

Bowling, Lawrence E., "Faulkner: Technique of 'The Sound and the Fury,'" *Kenyon Review,* X (Autumn, 1948), 552-66. A pioneering and still useful introduction to the technique. See also "Faulkner and the Theme of Innocence," *Kenyon Review,* XX (Summer, 1958), 466-87; "Faulkner and the Theme of Isolation," *Georgia Review,* XVIII (Spring, 1964), 50-66; and "Faulkner: The Theme of Pride in *The Sound and the Fury,*" *Modern Fiction Studies,* XI (Summer, 1965), 129-39.

Collins, Carvel, "The Interior Monologues of 'The Sound and the Fury,'" *English Institute Essays, 1952,* ed. Allen S. Downer (New York: Columbia University Press, 1954), pp. 29-56. Stresses debt of novel to Joyce, *Macbeth,* and Freud.

England, Martha W., "Quentin's Story: Chronology and Explication," *College English,* XXII (December, 1960), 228-35. A detailed attempt to order Quentin's past.

Meriwether, James B., "Notes on the Textual History of *The Sound and the Fury,*" *The Papers of the Bibliographical Society of America,* LVI (1962), 285-316. Adds insights into the novel's meaning as well as its history.

Millgate, Michael, *The Achievement of William Faulkner.* New York: Random House, 1966, pp. 94-111. Excellent discussion of novel's "twilight" qualities, with good examples (based on study of manuscript) of Faulkner's craft. Reprinted in *Faulkner: A Collection of Critical Essays,* ed. Robert Penn Warren. Englewood Cliffs, N.J.: Prentice-Hall, Inc., 1966, pp. 94-108.

Sartre, Jean-Paul, "On *The Sound and the Fury:* Time in the Work of Faulkner," in *Literary and Philosophical Essays,* trans. Annette Michelson. London: Rider & Co., 1955, pp. 79-87. An influential essay, first published in 1939. Reprinted in Warren, pp. 87-93.

Thompson, Lawrence, "Mirror Analogues in *The Sound and the Fury*," *English Institute Essays, 1952*, pp. 83-106. Reprinted in Warren, pp. 109-21. A good study of the relationship of imagery and theme.

Volpe, Edmond L., *A Reader's Guide to William Faulkner*. New York: Farrar, Straus and Giroux, 1964, pp. 87-125, 353-77. A concise and sensitive general analysis.

Young, James Dean, "Quentin's Maundy Thursday," *Tulane Studies in English*, X (1960), 143-51. A search for Christian symbolism.

TWENTIETH CENTURY VIEWS

American Authors